Exploring
Human Geography
with Maps

Second Edition

Margaret W. Pearce

Owen J. P

W. H. Freema

New

ISBN–13: 978-1-4292-2981-4
ISBN–10: 1-4292-2981-0

Maps and figures by Margaret W. Pearce unless otherwise indicated.

Printed in the United States of America

First Printing

W. H. Freeman and Company
41 Madison Avenue
New York, NY 10010
Houndsmills, Basingstoke
RG21 6XS, England
www.whfreeman.com

Contents

Introduction

This book of map exercises and activities introduces you, the geography student, to the diverse world of maps as a fundamental tool for exploring and presenting ideas in human geography. The book takes a thematic approach to the subject, exploring one geographic theme per chapter with exercises in map interpretation and construction.

The purpose of the exercises is to reinforce rather than repeat information from your textbook and class. Each map exercise applies fundamentals of human geography while also introducing map construction and interpretation skills.

Structure of Each Chapter

Each chapter begins with a vocabulary box listing the human geography terms you need to know to do the map exercises. This vocabulary is not defined in the exercises, so it will help to take a moment to review their meanings from your class and reading notes before starting the exercises.

Below the list of applied vocabulary is a list of new vocabulary applied in that chapter. You will see that there is more new vocabulary to learn in the earlier chapters; these taper off as you gradually master the basics.

Because the exercise chapters are intended to be completed in chronological order, later chapters build on the terminology and mapping skills of the earlier chapters. If you choose to dip into the book for short sections, or approach the topics in a different order, referring to these vocabulary boxes will help you locate unfamiliar concepts or Web sites as you proceed.

After the vocabulary boxes, each chapter (except the first and the last) proceeds with three map exercises exploring some of the themes from class. There are three modes of exercises, reflecting the three modes of the map as a tool for geographers. The mode of an exercise is shown at the beginning of the exercise by an icon so that you know which type of map exercise it is. (Some exercises explore more than one mode of the map and have two icons.) The three modes are:

✦ THE LANGUAGE OF MAPS

This mode introduces the fundamentals of map use and interpretation, such as scale, projections, data classification, and remote sensing, in human geographical contexts.

◎ VISUAL EXPLORATIONS

These exercises focus on using maps for exploring different representations of spatial data. Most of the exercises in this mode use interactive Web sites for data exploration. These exercises can be accessed through the W. H. Freeman Web site at **bcs.whfreeman.com/jordan11e**. To complete these exercises, you only need access to an Internet browser. Some of the URLs utilize java plug-ins and/or Adobe Acrobat Reader. Apart from these tools, however, no special software is needed.

☺ OTHER WAYS OF MAPPING

These exercises introduce maps approaching the theme from the perspective of another culture or period in history. The exploration and depiction of the human dimension through maps is not an invention of modern Western society, and there is much that can be learned by looking at how others have approached it.

For most of the exercises in the three modes, you will be interpreting maps and writing the answers on a separate piece of paper. In some instances, a map in the book is intended to be photocopied as part of the assignment, or you will be asked to print a page from a Web site. The book was designed to stay intact this way so that you can always refer back to maps and vocabulary in completed exercises, and so you can make use of the index.

In addition to access to the Internet and a photocopier, you will occasionally need to use a calculator for the exercises. There is no other special equipment required.

New to the Second Edition

This second edition includes ten new exercises that probe the relationship between mapmaking and human geography. In addition to these new exercises, the remaining exercises from the first edition have been thoroughly revised. These changes have brought deeper explorations of Geographic Information Systems, remote sensing, and the geographies of gender and ethnicity, natural hazards, the Internet infrastructure, and settlement density.

Why Only Maps?

Human geographers depend on all kinds of tools and materials beyond writing to do their work because the work itself is diverse. They need tools for interpreting human landscapes, for collecting and analyzing geographical information, and for presenting their findings to others. Maps permeate each of these stages of doing human geography, from initial source materials to exploration and analysis to communication of findings.

Rather than explore the spectrum of different methods and sources available to geographers, the focus here is on the map in all of its diverse applications. It is hoped that you will take away from these exercises a vision of mapping as rich, multifaceted, fluid, and fundamental to your awareness of human geography.

Maps for Human Geography

Vocabulary applied in this chapter
map
culture
material culture

New vocabulary
definitions and functions
  of the map
map symbols:
  mimetic and abstract

✹ ◑ 1.1
Maps and Culture

The task of the geographer is to investigate spatiality. But spatiality is an elusive concept to express. Often when we attempt to explain it in words, spatiality slips away. Words, whether spoken or written, are a linear mode of explaining, and as such are limited in their communication of spatial concepts.

Alternatively, if we attempt to explain a place with a picture, as in a drawing or a photograph, another limited dimension of spatiality is presented. Pictures capture one frame, one piece of space, but spatiality itself is fragmented by these frames. How does this frame relate to another frame? Where are the interconnections?

To overcome these limitations, geographers often use words and pictures together to approximate spatiality. But there is another way to both explore and express this spatiality — mapping.

As a visual medium, the **map** is one of the strongest tools for communicating spatiality. The characteristics of the map, especially its blending of scientific and artistic aspects, render it particularly useful for geography. Indeed, many people view the map as the most important tool that a geographer can learn to use. This chapter explores three aspects of the map that make it so useful.

Maps Show Location

Maps provide locational information — the first clues to understanding place. Maps show us the nature of the connections between those locations, how they are joined or separated. Connections allow us to stand back and see "the big picture" that may be invisible to us as we are standing in the landscape. For example, we may observe the distribution of phenomena over long distances, and the density and sparsity of things observable and physical or abstract and invisible.

Study the map on the facing page. This is a detail of the Door Peninsula region from the 1996 map, "Cultural Map of Wisconsin." The map portrays the cultural geography of the state through detailed geographical information and insets for the major cities. Each point symbol refers to a type of cultural feature by shape and color (the numbers refer the reader to an accompanying index booklet for information). Each symbol is defined in the map's legend.

Question 1: Reflect on the characteristics of culture from your textbook. What is culture? Make a list of the essential elements that comprise culture.

Question 2: How do you think the makers of the map define culture? What types of elements are included in their definition?

Question 3: Compare the cultural criteria from Questions 1 and 2. What elements are similar? What elements are different?

Question 4: Which elements of culture do you think would be most difficult to depict on a map?

In his classic work *Things Maps Don't Tell Us*, Armin Lobeck wrote that in order to understand the physical landscape, geographers must be able to interpret the physical processes behind the symbols on maps. The map presents the results but omits the process, and only through learning how to closely read the map can a geographer access the missing dimensions of the physical world.

➤ OG7	College or University
DA22	Festival
1A10	Hiking Trail
1R2	Historic Community
TA3	Historic Site
RA15	Lighthouse
CL5	Museum or Tour
F17	Park or Forest
OG11	Rustic Road
SA32	Writer

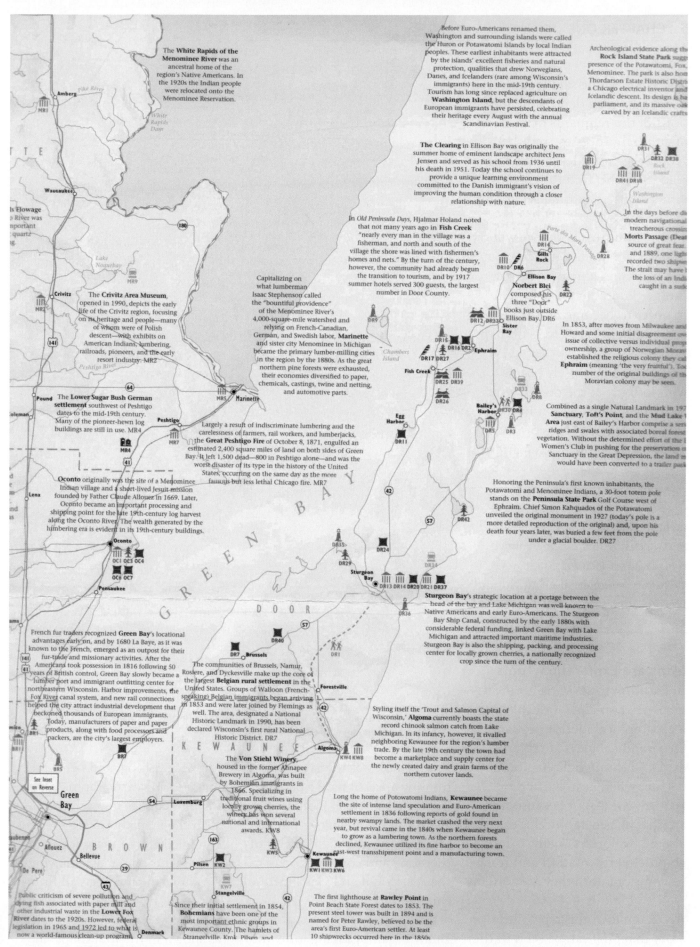

Detail (above) and legend (left) from "Cultural Map of Wisconsin" by David Woodward, Robert Ostergren, Onno Brouwer, Steven Hoelscher, and Joshua G. Hane. © 1996 University of Wisconsin Press. Used with permission.

The same can be said for culture. Often, the map depicts the locations of the remnants or artifacts of cultural processes, and the geographer must learn how to read closely to find the missing dimensions of cultural geography.

Throughout this book, we will try to push the limits between what can be *seen* in a map and what can be *gleaned from what is seen*, in order to become more adept users and critical viewers of maps.

Part of reading closely begins with looking at the overall pattern of elements shown in the map and in the connections between elements in the pattern.

Question 5: Look again at the elements depicted in the Door Peninsula map, focusing this time on connections between locations. Can you glean any information about cultural processes from these connections?

Maps are Exploration Tools
In addition to showing location, maps are also tools for exploring a geographical idea or problem. Geographical ideas are often explored through discussion and debate, whether in written or spoken words. But because they are spatial, geographical ideas can also be explored visually, through graphic representation and rerepresentation, until they are solved.

An example of this type of exploratory mapping can be seen in the maps collected by Hugh Brody in British Columbia in 1978.

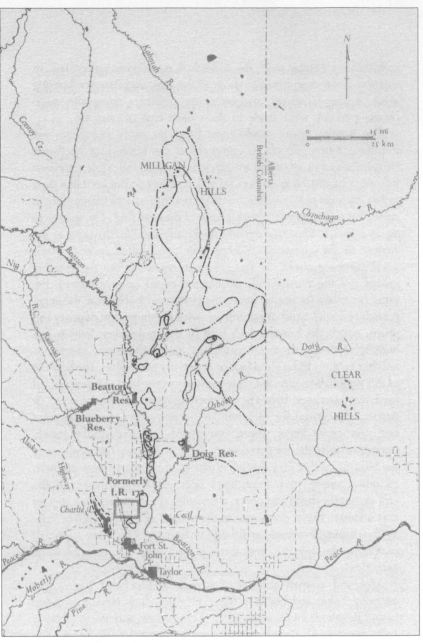

"Doig River Reserve: One Hunter's Land-Use Biography," from *Maps and Dreams: Indians and the British Columbia Frontier* by Hugh Brody. Prospect Heights, Ill.: Waveland Press, 1997. Used with permission of the author. Map by Karen Ewing.

Brody's task was to map the hunting areas of native people in northern British Columbia, as part of a federal government effort to anticipate the effects of the siting and construction of the Alaska Oil and Gas Pipeline through the region.

Brody began by asking individuals to mark on maps the boundaries of the lands they used for hunting, fishing, and berry-picking, creating cartographic hunting biographies for each person, as in the map above. He then compiled all the maps for each activity into one map, showing all berry-picking territory, all hunting territory, and all fishing territory, as overlapping boundaries, as shown in the four maps on page 7.

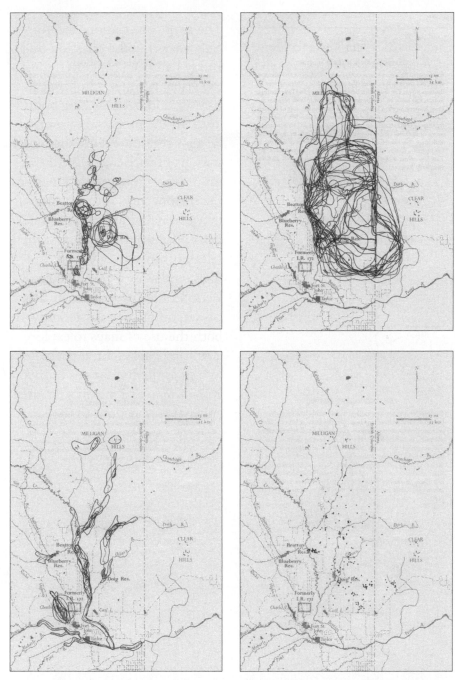

Clockwise from top left: "Doig River Reserve: Berry Picking Areas," "Doig River Reserve: Hunting," "Doig River Reserve: Camping Sites," "Doig River Reserve: Fishing Areas," from *Maps and Dreams: Indians and the British Columbia Frontier* by Hugh Brody. Prospect Heights, Ill.: Waveland Press, 1997. Used with permission of the author. Maps by Karen Ewing.

Question 6: What are the factors defining culture in this region? What aspect of those factors is depicted in the map?

Question 7: Compare the map "biography" with the activity maps. What do you think is the difference between the spatiality of culture as it is manifested in the activities of an individual versus culture as it is manifested in the activities of a community?

Later, Brody compiled the activity maps into a base map showing the outline of the estimated total area required for sustenance by each of the reserves, shown below.

Question 8: What kind of cultural information was ultimately lost in the final, compiled map?

The map compilations technically answered the question that Brody had been hired to find, the visual picture of hunting, fishing, and berry-picking boundaries. In the process, however, he also began to realize the limitations of such maps to communicate other cultural forces in the region, such as the tension between native and nonnative perceptions of the land, and the relationship among people, animals, and seasons. Brody's recollection of his experience in British Columbia is a classic study of both the use of maps to explore a cultural geographical problem, as well as the limitations of this type of map as a means to convey cultural connections to the land.

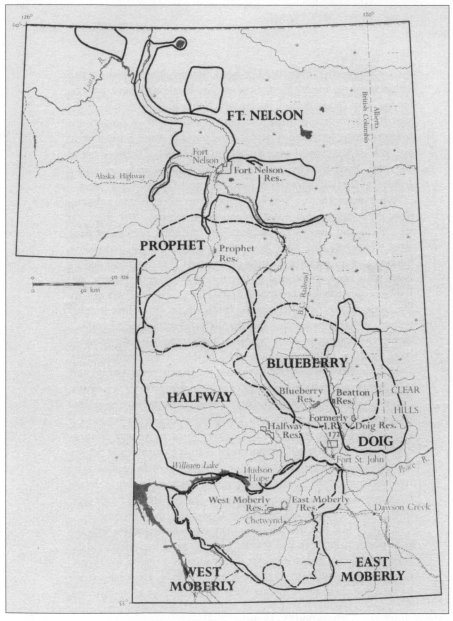

"Indian Hunting Territories in Northeast British Columbia," from *Maps and Dreams: Indians and the British Columbia Frontier* by Hugh Brody. Prospect Heights, Ill.: Waveland Press, 1997. Used with permission of the author. Map by Karen Ewing.

Maps are Material Culture

Finally, maps are also interesting to geographers because they are themselves **material culture** or **cultural evidence.** Maps locate and explore culture, and at the same time are a part of culture. As material culture, maps are primary sources that can graphically portray the perceptions, priorities, conventions, and aesthetics of a people.

A map does not merely record a landscape, it records the mapmaker's perception of that landscape, and the mapmaker's effort to shape our understanding. The mapmaker is shaped by culture. As a result, the map is not only a means of interpreting the cultural landscape, but also, as an artifact, is itself a part of that cultural landscape.

Because cultures differ greatly from one another, the look of the maps that each culture produces is also marked by great contrast. The differences in the way cultures perceive and represent the world are reflected in every element of the map: the amount of detail shown, the direction in which the map is oriented, the proportion of words versus graphics in the map, even the way the map symbols are conceived and drawn.

For example, we can find many cultural clues by studying the legend of a map. A map's legend often defines those features considered most significant by the mapmaker or institution behind the map. The legend above is

"Symbols for Village Maps," from *Maya Atlas: The Struggle to Preserve Maya Land in Southern Belize,* © 1997 North Atlantic Books. Used with permission of the publisher.

from the 1997 *Maya Atlas,* a collection of maps drawn by the Maya People of Southern Belize, depicting 36 Mayan communities. The goal of the atlas was to clearly represent Mayan lands without using the maps of other governments as a base, in order to establish a legal basis for indigenous land rights and land claims in the region.

Question 9: Based on the symbols defined in the legend, what assumptions would you make about daily life in Southern Belize? How do people make a living? What do they do for entertainment?

Question 10: Based on this legend, what assumptions would you make about the physical landscape?

Map symbols can vary dramatically from culture to culture. Every culture has a different sense of how **mimetic** a map symbol should be, that is, to what degree the symbol should resemble the object it represents, or by contrast how **abstract** a symbol should be. (For example, to symbolize a campground on a map, a tent would be a mimetic symbol, and a dot or square would be an abstract symbol.) The level of abstraction may vary within a culture, too, because cultures develop different types of maps to serve different needs in their societies.

The illustration on the right depicts a selection of symbols from Mesoamerican (both Mixtec and Aztec) cartography. On page 11, a selection of symbols from the U.S. Geological Survey topographical map series is shown for comparison. The two examples are not "map symbols" in quite the same sense of the term. The Aztecs used a pictographic, not an alphanumeric, writing system, so unlike Western map symbols, their map symbols are both the symbol and place-name combined. But we can still make comparisons based on the functions of the map symbols.

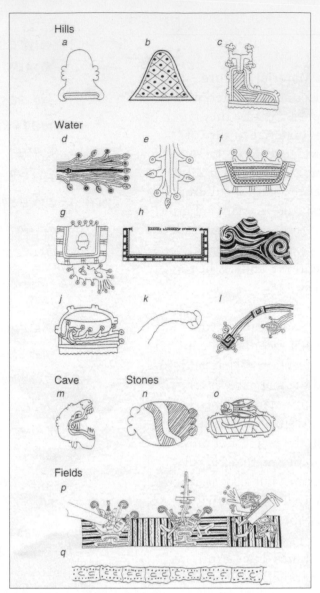

"Mesoamerican Cartography," from *History of Cartography, Vol. 2, Book 3: Cartography in the Traditional African, American, Arctic, Australian, & Pacific Societies,* © 1998 University of Chicago Press. Used with permission of the publisher.

Question 11: Compare the symbols from the Maya Atlas on page 9 to the Mesoamerican symbols, above, and the U.S. Geological Survey symbols, right. Each symbol set comes from a different culture's cartographic "language." Which symbol set is the most abstract? Which is the most mimetic?

Question 12: Are there wide differences in abstract and mimetic symbols in the same symbol set? Why do you think this is?

Question 13: All three cultures' symbol sets have a symbol for "cave." How do they compare?

Question 14: Does a comparison of the symbol for "cave" across three cultures give any clues to those cultures' different perceptions of the natural world? Why or why not?

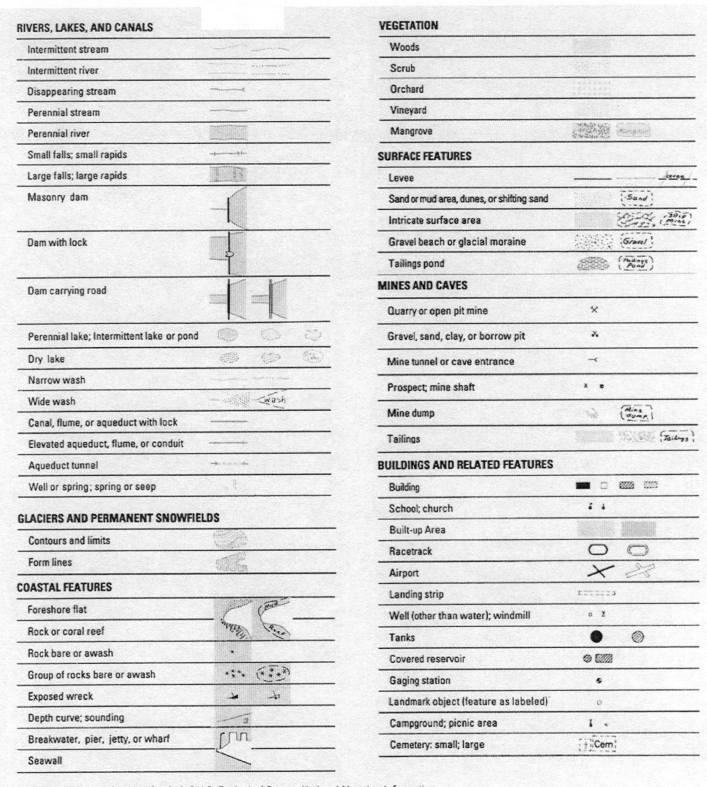

RIVERS, LAKES, AND CANALS

Intermittent stream	
Intermittent river	
Disappearing stream	
Perennial stream	
Perennial river	
Small falls; small rapids	
Large falls; large rapids	
Masonry dam	
Dam with lock	
Dam carrying road	
Perennial lake; Intermittent lake or pond	
Dry lake	
Narrow wash	
Wide wash	
Canal, flume, or aqueduct with lock	
Elevated aqueduct, flume, or conduit	
Aqueduct tunnel	
Well or spring; spring or seep	

GLACIERS AND PERMANENT SNOWFIELDS

Contours and limits	
Form lines	

COASTAL FEATURES

Foreshore flat	
Rock or coral reef	
Rock bare or awash	
Group of rocks bare or awash	
Exposed wreck	
Depth curve; sounding	
Breakwater, pier, jetty, or wharf	
Seawall	

VEGETATION

Woods	
Scrub	
Orchard	
Vineyard	
Mangrove	

SURFACE FEATURES

Levee	
Sand or mud area, dunes, or shifting sand	
Intricate surface area	
Gravel beach or glacial moraine	
Tailings pond	

MINES AND CAVES

Quarry or open pit mine	
Gravel, sand, clay, or borrow pit	
Mine tunnel or cave entrance	
Prospect; mine shaft	
Mine dump	
Tailings	

BUILDINGS AND RELATED FEATURES

Building	
School; church	
Built-up Area	
Racetrack	
Airport	
Landing strip	
Well (other than water); windmill	
Tanks	
Covered reservoir	
Gaging station	
Landmark object (feature as labeled)	
Campground; picnic area	
Cemetery: small; large	

Detail from "Topographic Map Symbols," U.S. Geological Survey, National Mapping Information, http://mac.usgs.gov/mac/isb/pubs/booklets/symbols/index.html.

Sources and Suggested Reading

Maps and Culture

Brody, Hugh. *Maps and Dreams: Indians and the British Columbia Frontier*. Prospect Heights, Ill.: Waveland Press, 1997.

Godlewska, Anne. "The Idea of the Map," in Susan Hanson (ed.). *Ten Geographic Ideas that Changed the World*. New Brunswick, N.J.: Rutgers University Press, 1997, pp. 17–39.

Lobeck, Armin K. *Things Maps Don't Tell Us*. Chicago: University of Chicago Press, 1960.

MacEachren, Alan M. *Some Truth with Maps: A Primer on Symbolization and Design*. Washington, D.C.: Association of American Geographers, 1994.

Mundy, Barbara E. "Mesoamerican Cartography," in David Woodward and G. Malcolm Lewis (eds.). *History of Cartography, Volume 2, Book 3: Cartography in the Traditional African, American, Arctic, Australian, and Pacific Societies*. Chicago: University of Chicago Press, 1998.

Toledo Maya Cultural Council. *Maya Atlas: The Struggle to Preserve Maya Land in Southern Belize*. Berkeley, Calif.: North Atlantic Books, 1997.

Woodward, David. "Cultural Map of Wisconsin." [map] 1:500,000. Madison, Wis.: University of Wisconsin Press, 1996.

2

Cultural Difference

Vocabulary applied in this chapter
folk culture
popular culture

New vocabulary
map scale:
  large-scale map
  small-scale map
representative fraction (RF)
map perspective:
  plan, oblique, profile
popular cartography
folk cartography

✳ 2.1
Scale and Cultural Evidence

One of the most fundamental pieces of information that a geographer needs to know about a map to decide if it will make a good source is **map scale.** Map scale, because it is inextricably tied to detail, often determines the type of cultural information that can be extracted from the map.

A **large-scale** map covers a small surface area in high detail. A typical large-scale map might include local roads, building footprints, vegetation, or elevation.

A **small-scale** map is the opposite: it covers a large surface area in low detail. A typical small-scale map would show major highways as lines, towns and cities as points, or whole continents or hemispheres.

Scale can be represented on a map with a bar for measuring lengths or as a statement, as in: "one inch equals five miles."

Scale can also be represented by a **representative fraction,** or **RF,** which tells you the ratio of the relationship of the map to earth. In other words, an RF of 1:10,000 means that 1 length of anything on the map equals 10,000 of those same lengths on the earth: 1 inch on the map would equal 10,000 inches on the earth, 1 millimeter on the map would equal 10,000 millimeters on the earth, and 1 handlength

on the map would equal 10,000 handlengths on the earth.

In the language of the RF, anything that is 1:25,000 scale or larger is considered "large scale." Anything 1:250,000 scale or smaller is considered "small scale." (And everything in the middle is "medium.")

The scale of a map, whether it is large or small, can be a good indicator of the type of geographical information that you will find in the map. Consider two examples from the Ordnance Survey map series from the United Kingdom. The map below is 1:63,360, which seems to be an odd RF, until you translate it to the equivalent verbal statement: "one inch

equals one mile." A map of the same area on the opposite page is 1:25,000. Between 1:63,360 and 1:25,000, the difference in the amount of geographical detail that can be shown is great.

Question 1: Study the geographical features of the 1:25,000 map. What kinds of transportation routes are depicted? What kinds of features are named? Are there any indicators of the type of economic activity in this region?

Question 2: Compare your reading to the smaller-scale 1:63,360 map below. What features are preserved in both maps? What information is lost in the smaller-scale map?

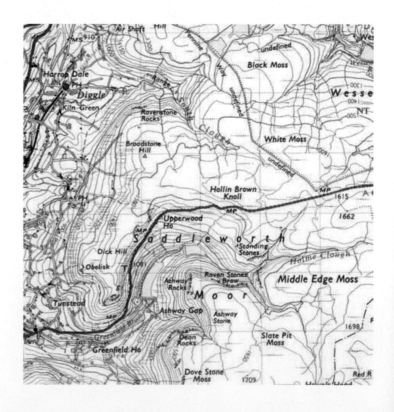

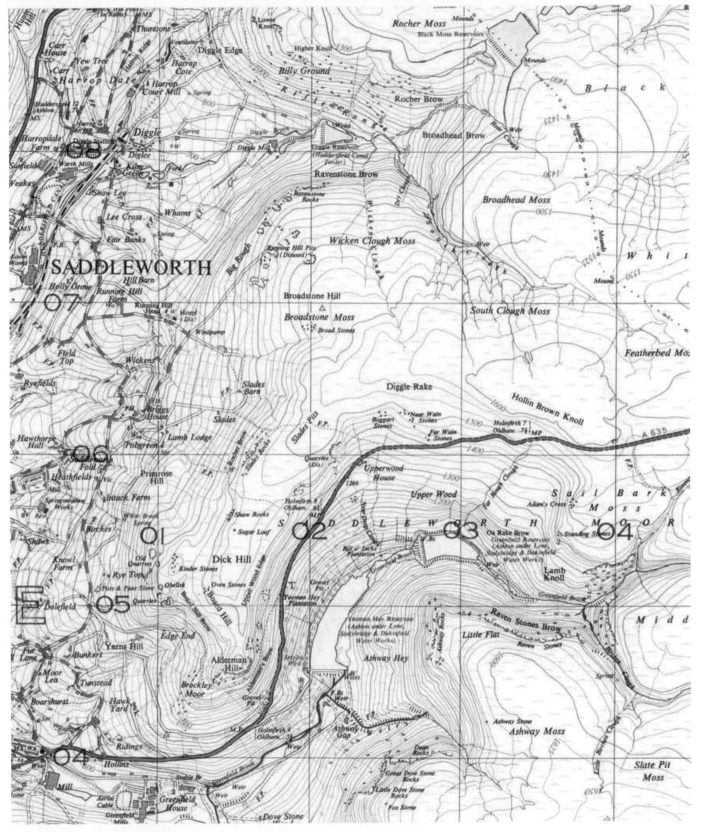

Left: Detail from "Huddersfield," 1961. Above: detail from "Saddleworth," 1957. Both images reproduced from Ordnance Survey mapping on behalf of The Controller of Her Majesty's Stationery Office, © Crown Copyright. License Number MC 100037914.

Question 3: How would your impression of this region be different if you had only the 1:63,360 map to work with?

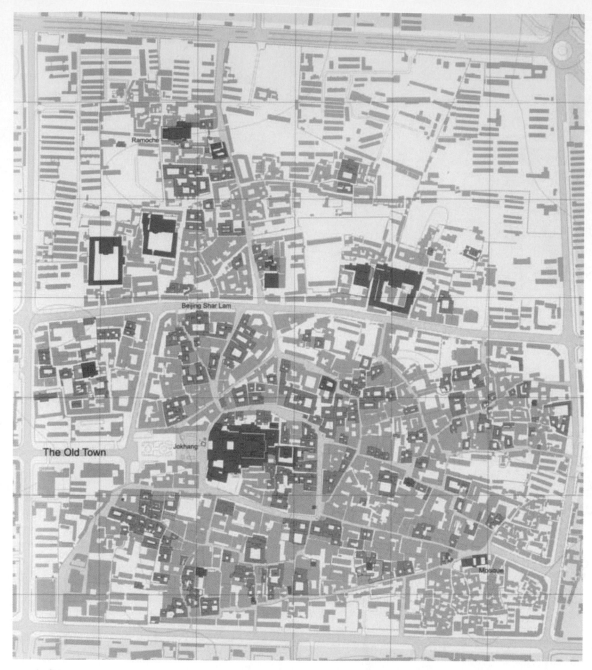

Detail of "General map of the LHCA project, 1999," from *The Lhasa Atlas: Traditional Tibetan Architecture and Townscape,* © 2001 Knud Larsen and Amund Sinding Larsen. Used with permission of the author and the publisher.

Finding Parallel Worlds in the Large-Scale Map

Large-scale maps are a useful way to look for examples of the parallel worlds of **folk culture** and **popular culture** because large-scale maps have more potential to show material culture than do small-scale maps.

In this map of the ancient city of Lhasa, Tibet, we can explore these parallel worlds. Looking at the city at an RF of 1:7,500,

the patterns of city streets and buildings are clearly visible. Modern architecture is depicted in gray. Traditional architecture is depicted in dark orange, signifying religious buildings, and light orange, signifying secular buildings. Tibetan urban form is differentiated from modern city planning by certain characteristics, including orientation of buildings to the south; use of circular structure to emphasize a center focal point (rather than the West-

ern structural tradition of a linear line of sight terminating at a focal point); and curved rather than straight paths and roads.

The map was compiled by the Lhasa Historical City Atlas Project as part of an effort both to document the rapidly changing Lhasa architectural pattern from traditional Tibetan to modern Chinese, and to establish a basis for Tibetan architectural preservation. In Lhasa, as in many of

Clockwise from top left: "New Cinema building," "New Market Hall," and "Tsonak Lam," by Knud Larsen, © 2001. From *The Lhasa Atlas: Traditional Tibetan Architecture and Townscape* by Knud Larsen and Amund Sinding Larsen. Used with permission of the author and the publisher.

the world's old cities, the ancient vernacular architecture is at risk of being replaced with modern buildings. The Lhasa photos on this page show the difference between the modern architecture of China (top left) and the vernacular architecture of Tibet (below left). The photo above, right shows how the two types of built landscapes parallel each other at a marketplace.

A look at the map on the opposite page immediately shows the parallel traditional (orange) and modern (grey) parts of the city. But even without the benefits of color coding, closer study of the map reveals many indicators of the parallel worlds.

Question 4: What differences in the shapes and sizes of the streets indicate differences between vernacular and modern?

Question 5: Are there differences in the orientation of streets and buildings, which would also indicate vernacular or modern landscapes? Explain why you think they are similar or different.

Question 6: The photographs on this page illustrate the differences in the two architectural styles. Can you also see differences between the two styles in the map? If so, how do these differences compare to what is shown in the photographs?

Much of the Lhasa folk landscape has already been covered over by modernity. For example, many of the ancient concentric pilgrimage routes, called koras, are now part of the relic landscape. The koras are the old circular paths that form concentric circles around the major temples.

Question 7: Where in the map can you find the relic patterns of the koras? What aspects of the built environment reveal the locations of these earlier paths?

⊕ ◑ 2.2
Putting It All in Perspective

Like map scale, **map perspective** is another characteristic that determines the type of geographical information that can be portrayed in a map. Perspective is the term that cartographers use to describe the angle from which a map or image is viewed. All maps present the landscape from a particular angle for the viewer, though as viewers we may not always be aware of it.

A map that presents the landscape as if we are looking straight down on it from above is called a **plan** view. This is the conventional perspective view of a map, as shown in the early U.S. Geological Survey map of St. Paul, Minnesota on the lower half of the opposite page.

Because the U.S. Geological Survey publishes several editions of the same map over time, to account for changes in both the physical and built landscapes, geographers often draw on several editions of the same map sheet to visualize geographical change in a given area.

A map that presents the landscape as if we are looking down upon it from above, at a slight angle, is called an **oblique** or **bird's-eye view.** The image at the top of the opposite page depicts St. Paul from an oblique perspective.

Question 1: What geographical information is unique to the oblique perspective? To the plan perspective?

Question 2: Are there any geographical elements that are downplayed or hidden by oblique perspective? Explain.

Question 3: How does the plan perspective map influence your perception of the elements noted in Question 2? In other words, does the plan perspective provide a more balanced view of the city, or does it emphasize and deemphasize elements in the same way as the oblique?

Perspective in Pop Culture

As it turns out, the use of the oblique perspective tends to be a technique common to **popular cartography**, that is, the maps of material popular culture.

For example, oblique perspectives of cities and towns, the so-called urban views or bird's eye views, were mass-produced in the United States during the late nineteenth century. Several thousand American cities and towns were represented in view form by a number of artists, lithographers, and entrepreneurs, many of whom remain anonymous. The views were ubiquitous, displayed on the walls of homes and businesses across the country.

Anonymous. *St. Paul, Minn., January, 1888*. J. H. Mahler Co., 1888. Minnesota Historical Society (MR2.9–SP1e–p10). Used with permission of Minnesota Historical Society.

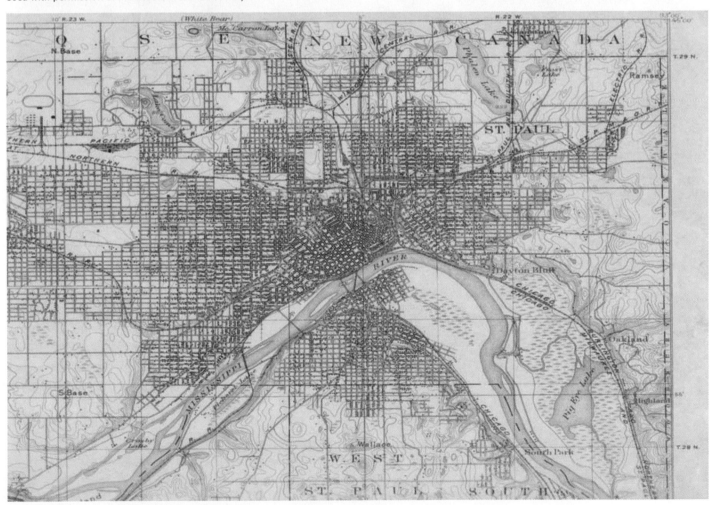

U.S. Geological Survey. *St. Paul.* 1896 ed., rep. 1917.

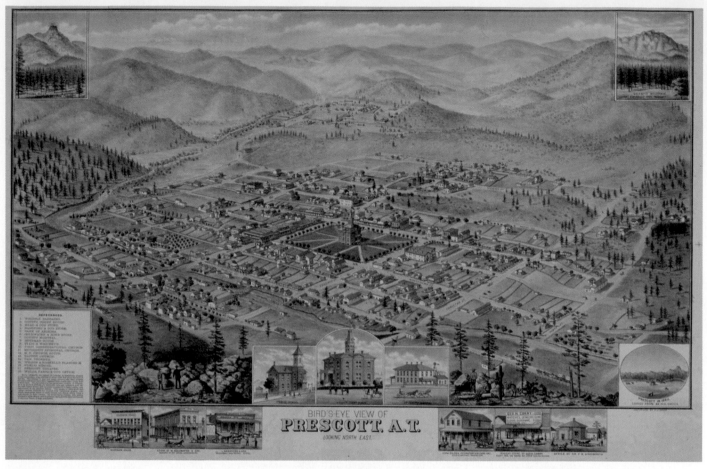

Bird's-Eye View of Prescott, A.T. Looking North East. Chromolithograph, after C.J. Dyer, 1885. Collection of the Amon Carter Museum, Fort Worth, Texas, #1968.45. Used with permission of the Amon Carter Museum.

Above are bird's-eye views for two Western cities, Prescott, Arizona, and Reno, Nevada. Both towns are laid out in a grid structure, with a river running through the town. Their depiction in each of the views, however, is slightly different.

These two views include a third type of perspective, called the **profile view.** A map or image that presents the landscape as if we are standing before it, viewing it at eye level, is a profile view. Although we don't usually think of a profile perspective as a "map," the profile is commonly used in popular cartography in conjunction with the oblique and planar perspectives.

In these two views, the center of the image presents the city in oblique perspective; in the margins, details about the city are presented in profile perspective.

Oblique and profile perspectives seem to depart from the conventional idea of the map. But a careful reading of these two views will begin to reveal the ways in which bird's-eye views could be useful to human geographers.

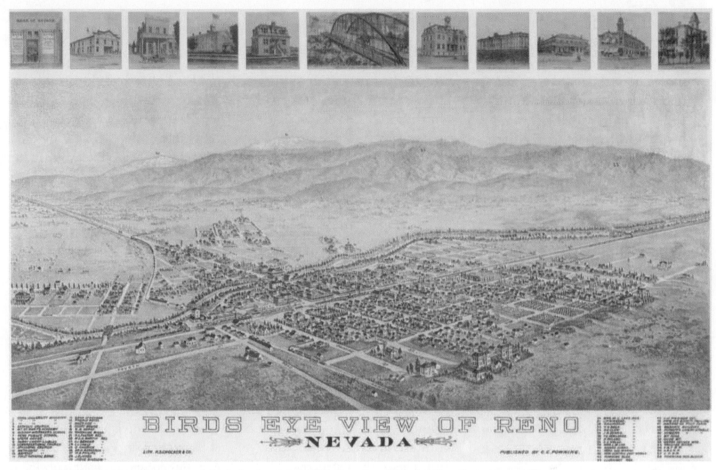

Anonymous. *Birds Eye View of Reno Nevada.* H. S. Crocker & Co.: 1885. Courtesy of Historic Urban Plans, Ithaca, N.Y.

Question 4: What elements of each city are placed in the foreground in these two maps? What elements are placed in the background?

Question 5: What is the difference in the type of information shown in profile in the two views? How does that influence your perception of the city?

❶ 2.3
Folk Cartography

In Western society, maps are more often the purveyors of popular culture than folk culture. Indeed, many critics have bemoaned the fact that, although the map evokes the landscape of folklife, the folk landscape cannot actually be found there. But one way to find folklife in maps is to go to the maps created by folk cultures.

An interesting example can be seen in the nineteenth-century Shaker communities of the Northeast United States. The Shaker movement began in upstate New York in the 1780s and spread throughout the eastern United States during the 1800s. Shaker faith emphasized communal living, simplicity, confession, pacifism, and the equality of human beings as the virtues that would bring them closer to God. In their arts, Shakers discouraged decoration for decoration's sake as an unspiritual practice that clouded the spiritual path. Instead, Shaker artisans nurtured a practical, symmetrical aesthetic in order to create works both useful to the community and religiously instructive.

In his book *Shaker Village Views*, Robert P. Emlen provides a comprehensive look at the maps that came out of Shaker folklife. Emlen explains that to manage the communal resources of a Shaker village, a vernacular cartography evolved over time that met the need for both an archived record for the community and a status report to be sent back to the parent ministry.

In each village, one of the men, or "brethren," had the responsibility of making a map that would show the overall plan of the town, the architecture of buildings, and the layout and pattern of planted fields and orchards. To remain within the aesthetic framework of their faith, these mapmakers strove to create detailed, but not decorative, cartography.

On page 23 is an example of a map by Brethren Henry Clay Blinn, known as "Br. Henry," of Canterbury, New Hampshire.

Question 1: Think about the content of the map. What can be gleaned from this document about daily life in the Shaker world? What kinds of agricultural activities could be found in this village?

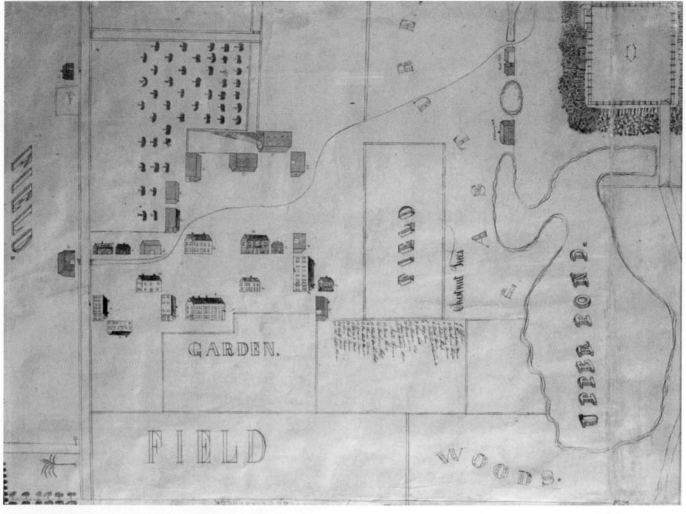

Map of Canterbury, New Hampshire by Brethren Henry Clay Blinn. Courtesy of Canterbury Shaker Village Archives, Canterbury, N.H. Copywork by Bill Finney, 2001-2002.

Now turn your attention to the way this map was drawn. As in popular cartography, map perspective is often used in folk cartography to communicate certain aspects of geography.

Question 2: How has Br. Henry used map perspective? Is this a plan, oblique, or profile view? How does this differ from what you would expect to see on a conventional topographical map?

Question 3: Why do you think he uses perspective in this way? What elements of the folk landscape are represented as a result?

Question 4: In which direction is the map oriented? Why would this be useful?

Question 5: Shaker artists valued words and images equally as tools for artistic representation. Does Br. Henry use words in his maps differently than the way words are used in an Ordnance Survey map, or a U.S. Geological Survey map? Explain your reasoning.

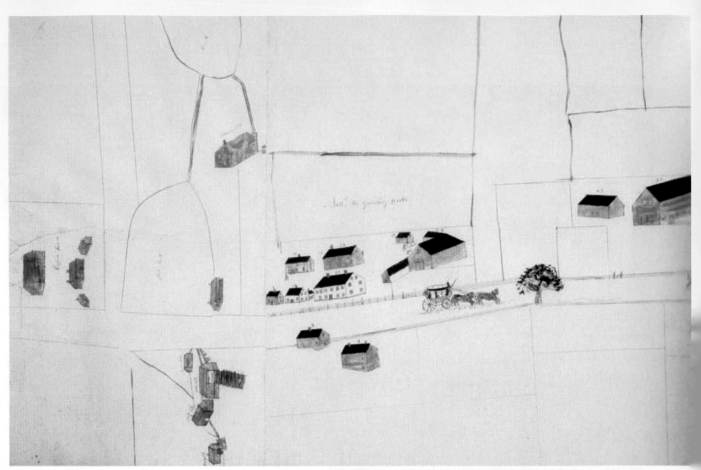

Detail of *Poland, Maine* by Brethren Joshua H. Bussell. Used with permission, United Society of Shakers, Sabbathday Lake, Maine, and Robert P. Emlen.

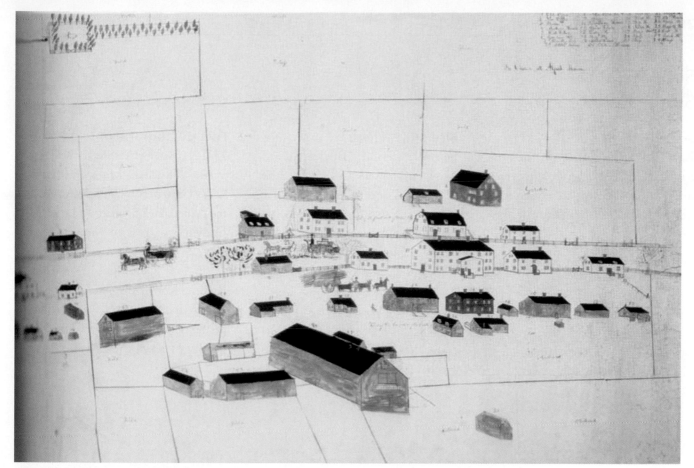

The Shaker Village at Alfred, Maine by Brethren Joshua H. Bussell. Courtesy of the Museum of Fine Arts, Boston. Gift of Dr. J.J.G. McCue, 1978.461.

Compare Br. Henry's map to two maps by Brethren Joshua H. Bussell, one depicting the Shaker community at Alfred, Maine, and the other depicting the Shaker community at Poland Hill, Maine.

Question 6: How does Br. Joshua use perspective? How does his use of perspective shape what is depicted for Alfred, Maine?

Question 7: How does Br. Joshua use symbols for geographical features in his maps?

Sources and Suggested Readings

Scale

Larsen, Knud, and Amund Sinding-Larsen. *The Lhasa Atlas: Traditional Tibetan Architecture and Townscape.* Boston: Shambhala, 2001.

Bird's-Eye Views

Danzer, Gerald. "Bird's-Eye Views of Towns and Cities," in David Buisseret (ed.). *From Sea Charts to Satellite Images: Interpreting North American History through Maps.* Chicago: University of Chicago Press, 1990, pp. 143–63.

Reps, John W. *Bird's Eye Views: Historic Lithographs of North American Cities.* New York: Princeton Architectural Press, 1998.

Folk Cartography

Emlen, Robert P. *Shaker Village Views: Illustrated Maps and Landscape Drawings by Shaker Artists of the Nineteenth Century.* Hanover: University Press of New England, 1987.

Ryden, Kent. *Mapping the Invisible Landscape: Folklore, Writing, and the Sense of Place.* Iowa City: University of Iowa Press, 1993.

CHAPTER

3

Population

Vocabulary applied in this chapter
geodemography
total fertility rate (TFR)
infant mortality rate
Human Development
   Index (HDI)
Human Poverty Index (HPI-1)
age distribution
population pyramid

New vocabulary
choropleth map
quantiles
Gender-related Development
   Index (GDI)
sprawl
dweller density map
isarithmic map
worker density map

🔍 3.1
Global Trends of Natality and Standard of Living

Human geographers are particularly interested in **geodemography** because the description ("graphy") of where on earth ("geo") people ("demos") are located is central to their interest in the spatial dimensions of human life. Geodemography is among the most commonly mapped themes because governments, international organizations, and nongovernmental organizations (NGOs) are all interested in the spatial distribution of humans: where they are, how many there are, and what they are like.

Mapping geodemographic data allows us to see patterns and relationships that would otherwise be lost in the jumble of population numbers in a table, giving us more insight into the population dynamics of the region. These mappable data are commonly referred to as population indicators, and they include such measures as **total fertility rate (TFR), infant mortality rate,** and the **Human Development Index.** This exercise gets you started comparing population indicators at a global scale, and then examining the details regionally.

One Web site where you can explore geodemography is the United Nations Environment Programme (UNEP)'s "GEO Data Portal." In addition to the numerous environmental databases available here, this site allows you to explore a number of different population indicators.

Step 1 Launch your browser and navigate to the "GEO Data Portal" link under Exercise 3.1 in the "Exploring Human Geography with Maps" section of the *Human Mosaic* Web site. This will take you to the main page for the GEO Data Portal, shown here.

First, let's focus on the TFR data.

Question 1: Reflect on what you learned in class about TFR. In which regions or countries do you expect to find a TFR much lower than 2.1? Where do you expect to find a TFR that is much greater than 2.1?

Step 2 Under "search the GEO Database," enter the words "fertility rate," and click "Search." You should now see a set of available database options relevant to "fertility rate."

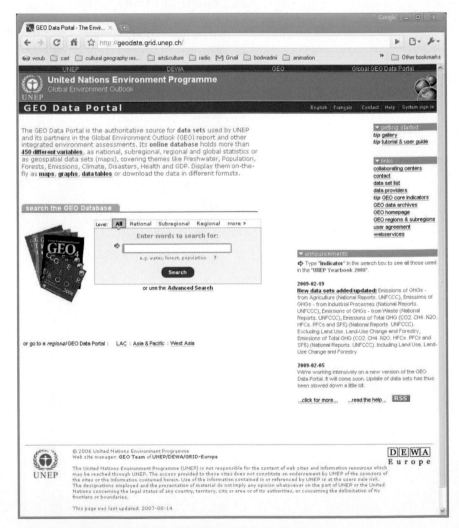

Screenshot from GEO Data Portal, UNEP 2009. Used with permission.

Step 3   Choose the top data option, fertility at the national level, by clicking on the radio button and then clicking "continue."

Step 4   From the year selections, check the box labeled "Select All" next to the list of available years, and then click "continue."

You should now be looking at a list of available output options for the data, as shown here.

As a data "portal," the GEO Data Portal offers data to view in a map, chart, or table, as well as to download for use in statistical or mapping packages.

Step 5   Under "Draw Map," click on the image of the map. This will open up a separate window with a global **choropleth map** showing estimated fertility rate for the years 2045–2050. A choropleth map shows geographical information over an area, in this case, assigning a color for each country based on the data for that country.

Question 2: Which regions have projected TFR estimates greater than 2.1? How does this compare with your answer to question 1, above?

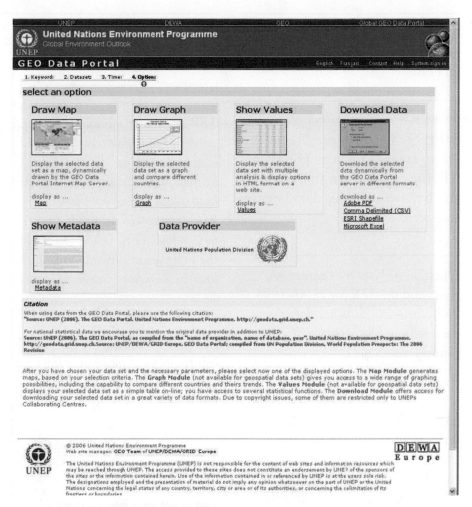

Screenshot from GEO Data Portal, UNEP 2009. Used with permission.

Step 6   Click the "Trend Analysis" tab in the red "Theme" box and check the "Calculate difference" option. Choose to look at the difference between 1990–1995 and 2005–2010, and display the difference "in percent."

Step 7   Now, click the "Classification" tab next to the "Trend Analysis" tab. Change the classification scheme by clicking the radio button for "Quantiles" and then clicking "update map."

Although the data set has not changed, the choropleth display is now quite different. In a **quantiles** classification scheme, data classes are comprised of an equal number of observations. (For more about classification schemes, and the strengths and limitations of each one, see Chapter 5.)

Step 8   Click "update map" to see your results.

Question 3: In which countries or regions do you see the greatest change in TFR?

Step 9 Click on the "Table" tab to access a table of TFR data. Choose a country of interest to you (you will use this data later in the exercise, below).

Question 4: Note the country you chose and the TFR for 1990–1995 and 2000–2005. What does this data tell you about natality in the country you chose?

Step 10 Click the orange "new search" link to the right of the table. This should return you to GEO Data Portal Home. In the box, type "infant mortality rate" and click "Search."

Step 11 From "select a dataset," choose "Infant mortality rate—National," click "continue," again choose all years of the data, and click "continue."

Step 12 Draw your map as in Step 5, above.

Step 13 Using the options in the "General" tab, browse the estimated infant mortality rate between 1950 and 2050. Use your Zoom and Zoom Out tools to explore changes in infant mortality rate at the regional level.

Question 5: What regional patterns do you see?

Question 6: Reflect on what you know about the relationship between TFR and infant mortality rate when compared to population trends and standard of living. If you could look at these two data sets simultaneously, how would you expect them to correlate? In other words, for a country with a high TFR, would you expect the infant mortality rate to be high or low? Explain your reasoning.

Step 14 Click on the "Table" tab to access a table of infant mortality data, and locate the country you chose in Step 7, above.

Question 7: Note the infant mortality rates for 1990–1995 and 2000–2005. What does this data tell you about standard of living in the country you chose?

For another view of the population indicators, we turn to the International Data Base of the U.S. Census Bureau to see whether natality and standard of living are also reflected in the **population pyramids.**

Step 15 Navigate your browser to the "International Data Base (IDB) Population Pyramids" link under Exercise 3.1 in the "Exploring Human Geography with Maps" section of the *Human Mosaic* Web site. This will take you to the Pyramids page for the IDB, shown below.

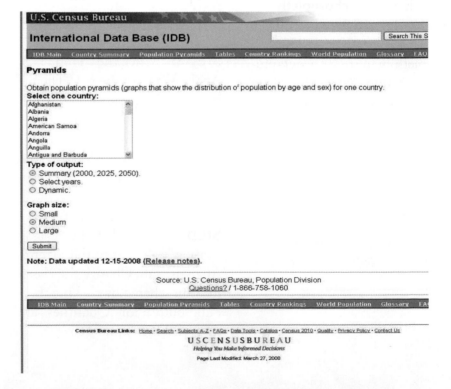

Screenshot from U.S. Census Bureau Web site, International Data Base (IDB), 2009.

Step 16   In the "Select one country" drop-down menu, select the country you chose in Step 7, above; for "Type of output:" click the radio button for "Select years"; for "Graph size:" click the radio button for "Large"; then hit "Submit."

Step 17   For the "IDB Population Pyramid Year Selection," select "1980," then hold down your "ctrl" key to also select "2000" and "2020." This will return an annual series of twelve population pyramids for your particular country.

Question 8: Analyze the changing shape of the population pyramid. Is this population shrinking, expanding, or remaining relatively constant? Is it a youthful population or an aging population?

Question 9: Look back at your notes for TFR and infant mortality rate for this country. Do the population pyramids echo the changes in the data tables? What are the clues in the shape of the pyramids that tell us about natality and standard of living in this particular place?

A Closer Look at Standard of Living

The GEO Data Portal also allows us to track geodemographic data more specifically at the level of countries and regions. In this section, we will shift from a generalized, global view of population

indicators to see how those generalizations play out at the regional level, in the Middle East.

Step 18   Return to GEO Data Portal Home by navigating your browser to the "GEO Data Portal" link under Exercise 3.1 in the "Exploring Human Geography with Maps" section of the *Human Mosaic* Web site. Once there, select the "national" level, enter "HPI" as your search term, and click "Search."

Step 19   From the list of datasets, select the radio button for **Human Poverty Index (HPI)—**

National, click "continue," accept the default year of 2003, and again click "continue." For "select an option," again choose "Draw Map."

The choropleth map displays the percent of people living in poverty, as measured by the HPI, for each country for 2003.

Step 20   Zoom to the region of the Middle East by clicking on the Zoom tool on the grey panel to the left of the map and dragging a box around the general area of the Middle East, as in the image below. You can make minor adjustments using the

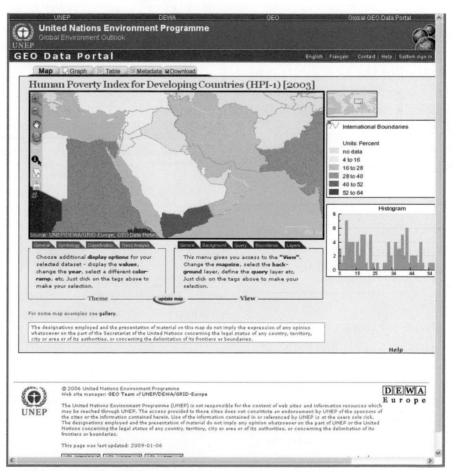

Screenshot from GEO Data Portal, UNEP 2009. Used with permission.

Zoom, Zoom Out, and Pan tools, until you have a good display of the choropleth map for the Middle East.

Step 21   Complete the map using the options in the blue "View" box below the map. Under the "Boundaries" tab, turn on the country labels by clicking the second box for "International Boundaries," as in the top image, below.

Next, make the country names black by clicking the "change properties" icon beside the second box, clicking the color fill option under "Label," and clicking "update," as in the bottom image.

Finally, under the "General" tab, choose a larger map size that fits your monitor (1200 × 600 if possible). To see your design changes, click the yellow oval for "Update Map." Your larger choropleth map should now be clearly labeled by country.

Question 10: Which Middle Eastern countries received the highest HPI rating, and which received the lowest?

Step 22   Print a copy of the map that you made for comparison later.

Step 23   Return to GEO Data Portal Home by clicking on the orange "new search" link to the

right of the map. Once there, select the "national" level, enter **"GDI"** as your search term, and click "Search."

The **Gender-related Development Index (GDI)** is another quality-of-life index developed by the UN. GDI re-examines the poverty indicators of HPI in terms of disparities between men and women, for example, illiteracy among men to illiteracy among women.

Step 24   Repeat Steps 20–23 to create a printed map of GDI in the Middle East.

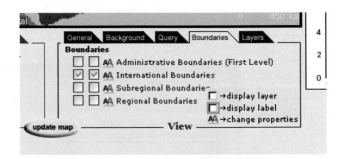

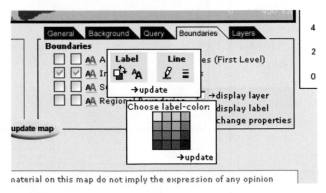

Screenshots from GEO Data Portal, UNEP 2009. Used with permission.

Question 11: What differences do you see in GDI within the Middle East?

Question 12: Look back at your printed copy of HPI ratings. How do they compare? Is there a general correlation by country between high ratings for HPI and high ratings for GDI, or does it vary depending on the particular country?

Question 13: From these particular measures, what might you conclude about disparities between men and women in the Middle East in 2003?

⊕ 3.2
The Regional Geography of Sprawl

In Exercise 3.1, you explored how population and standard of living are interrelated at a global level, and the ways in which high population levels, under particular political and economic conditions, can create disparities in the quality of life between men and women. Now, we turn to the question of population density and its impact on environmental conditions.

The **adaptive strategies** of overpopulation, when high population densities are consuming natural resources at high rates, may have environmentally unsustainable consequences. But low population densities, when combined with a high rate of natural resource consumption, can also be environmentally unsustainable. As you learned in Chapter 3 of your text, Americans consume about 25 percent of the world's natural resources, though they represent only 5 percent of the population.

One of the driving forces of this culture of consumption is **sprawl**. Although sprawl has many definitions, it is generally associated with the settlement conditions that occur when the rate at which a metropolitan area consumes land resources outpaces the rate of population increase in that area. The effects of sprawl on the environment, in addition to the increase in natural

resource consumption, include increases in air and water pollution, the loss of wildlife habitat, and loss of land in agriculture. The opposite of sprawling is **"densifying,"** the condition when population increase outpaces urban development of land in a metropolitan area.

In a 2001 report, the Center on Urban & Metropolitan Policy at the Brookings Institution found that sprawl is not ubiquitous across the United States, but characterized by strong regional differentiation. Southern and Northeastern cities, for example, are sprawling more than Western cities, though this runs counter to the common public perception that the West is a region of sprawling cities. These regional differences, the findings indicated, are created by certain factors, including the rapid population increase of a relatively small metropolitan population, an ethnic

geographic distribution with a low proportion of foreign-born residents and a high proportion of Hispanic residents, and a high proportion of land suitable for development (flat, privately owned, and with fewer wetland areas), among other criteria.

In this exercise, you will explore the cultural, political, and environmental characteristics of three cities—Atlanta, Las Vegas, and your own city—using the resources of the U.S. Census American FactFinder. Both Atlanta and Las Vegas are cities already associated with high rates of sprawl. But which is sprawling faster? And how do these rates compare to your own city?

Step 1   Launch your browser and navigate to the "American FactFinder" link under Exercise 3.2 in the "Exploring Human Geography with Maps" section of the *Human Mosaic* Web site. This will take you to the main page for the American Factfinder, shown here.

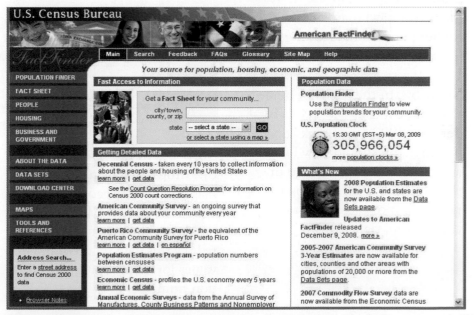

Screenshot from U.S. Census Bureau Web site, American FactFinder (http://factfinder.census.gov), 2009.

Step 2   Click on "Data Sets" in the column on the left, and choose the link "Decennial Census."

Step 3   In the new window, click the grey tab to activate "1990 Census," as shown top, right. In the section "1990 Summary Tape File 1 (STF 1)—100–Percent data," click the link "Thematic Maps." In census vocabulary, different types of data within a data set are called "themes" (hence "thematic maps").

Step 4   In the "Select geography" window, accept the default geographic type as "Nation" and geographic area as "United States," and click "Next," as in the middle, right.

For our first comparison, we will focus on the criteria that cities with fast rates of growth are likely to sprawl, and, in particular, cities with a lower population growing at a fast rate are more likely to sprawl than cities with higher populations growing at a fast rate.

Step 5   In the "Select Theme" window, choose "TM-P001. Total Persons: 1990," and click "Show Result." You should now have activated a choropleth map of the United States, showing the population of each state, as at the bottom, right.

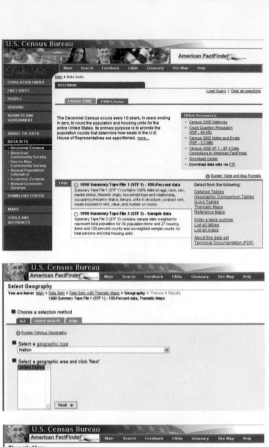

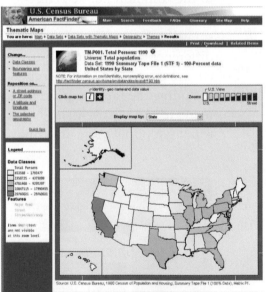

Screenshots from U.S. Census Bureau Web site, American FactFinder (http://factfinder.census.gov), 2009.

Step 6   In the "Display Map by:" drop-down menu above the map, change the geographic area from State to Metropolitan Area. The map should now redraw this data set according to values for metropolitan population numbers.

Step 7   In the "Click map to:" settings, click on the Identify tool. Then click your cursor over the metropolitan boundaries for Las Vegas, in the southern portion of Nevada, to activate a data pop-up window for that place.

Question 1: What was the population in 1990 for Las Vegas, NV MSA, according to the Census?

Step 8 Now use the Identify tool to look up the population densities for Atlanta, Georgia, and your own city. If you are not in a city that appears on this map, choose the metropolitan area closest to you.

Question 2: What is the 1990 population for Atlanta? For your city?

Step 9 From the "You are here:" toolbar at the top of your current Web page, click "Data Sets" to return to the Data Sets options, as in Step 2, above. This time, activate the "Census 2000" tab. Repeat Steps 3–8, above, to look up the populations of these three cities for 2000.

Question 3: What are the 2000 populations for these three cities?

Question 4: Which city began with a smaller population?

Question 5: Which city increased in population at a faster rate?

Question 6: Based on the criteria identified by the 2001 Brookings Institution report, which of these cities is more likely to sprawl?

Now explore the criteria for the ethnic geographies of these three cities. The 2001 report also found that urban populations with a low proportion of foreign-born residents and a high proportion of Hispanic residents are also cities likely to sprawl at a higher rate.

Step 10 Using the same tools from Steps 3–9, above, determine the Hispanic populations for each city in 1990 and 2000. For your data set, select "TM-P024. Percent of Persons Who Are of Hispanic Origin Excluding Cuban, Mexican or Puerto Rican."

Question 7: Which city has the highest proportion of Hispanic residents?

Step 11 Using the same tools from Steps 3–9, determine the foreign-born populations for each city in 1990 and 2000. For your data set, change to "Summary Tape File 3 (STF 3)— Sample data," and select "TM-P068. Percent of Persons Who are Foreign Born."

Question 8: Which city has the lowest proportion of foreign-born residents?

Question 9: Assess the geodemographic information you have collected for these three cities. Which city is most likely to sprawl, based on just these criteria?

Question 10: Do these criteria indicate that your city is likely to be sprawling or densifying? How does it compare to Atlanta and Las Vegas?

Question 11: Assess the report's emphasis on the connection between Hispanic population and sprawl. By isolating one sector of the population in this way, what do you think would be the consequences for people's perceptions of Hispanics?

The Visual Dimension of Sprawl

At the Lincoln Institute of Land Policy, Julie Campoli and Alex S. MacLean take a visual approach to sprawl. In their book, *Visualizing Density*, a city is interpreted as sprawling or densifying by measuring the number of housing units, or households, per acre, and comparing changes to those densities over time. By this definition, a measure of 3 to 5 units per acre would be considered a low-density, sprawling settlement landscape.

Like the Brookings Institution study, Campoli and MacLean use their measures of sprawl to overturn our visual perceptions of what sprawl looks like, in order to empower cities to visualize efficient development strategies at higher rates of densification.

For this last section, we will use their measuring tool to compare our interpretations of the population data earlier in the exercise.

Step 12   Navigate to the Census Bureau's "Density Using Land Area" link under Exercise 3.2 in the "Exploring Human Geography with Maps" section of the *Human Mosaic* Web site. This will take you to the main page for housing density statistics at the U.S. Census, shown in the screenshot at top, right.

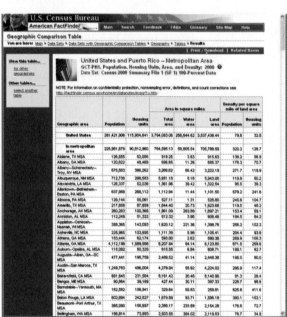

Screenshots from U.S. Census Bureau Web site, American FactFinder (http://factfinder.census.gov), 2009.

Step 13   Click on "Population, Housing Units, Area, and Density for Metropolitan Areas: 2000," to go to the table "GCT-PH1," as shown in the bottom screenshot.

Step 14 Use this table to look up the "Total area," in square miles, for the Atlanta and Las Vegas MSAs, as well as your own city, and record your results.

Step 15 Next, record the density of housing units for the Atlanta and Las Vegas MSAs, as well as your own city. These densities are calculated based on the land area, as opposed to the total area, of each MSA, and presented in housing units per square mile. To convert to housing units per acre, divide each figure by 640 and record your results.

Step 16 Hit the back button on your browser to return to the "Density Using Land Area" Web page, as in Step 12, above. Now, for each city, divide the housing units by acreage to find the number of housing units per acre for 1990 and 2000. This time, click on "Land Area, Population, and Density for Metropolitan Areas: 1990." You should now be at a Web page for "Table 2," as shown in the screenshot above, right.

Step 17 Use this table to look up the sizes, in square miles, for each of the three cities. Multiply each size by 640 to convert square miles to acres, and record your results.

```
Table 2.  Land Area, Population, and Density for Metropolitan Areas:  1990

(Metropolitan areas are as defined on June 30, 1990 for the 1990 Census.)

Source: U.S. Census Bureau
Released: March 14, 1996

                                   Pop. per Pop. per
Population  Sq.Km.   Sq.Mi.   Sq.Km.   Sq.Mi.  Name
---------------------------------------------------------------------------
---------------
    119655  2371.7    915.7     50.5    130.7  Abilene, TX MSA
    112561  1775.4    685.5     63.4    164.2  Albany, GA MSA
    874304  8413.6   3248.5    103.9    269.1  Albany-Schenectady-Troy, NY MSA
    480577  3020.4   1166.2    159.1    412.1  Albuquerque, NM MSA
    131556  3425.7   1322.7     38.4     99.5  Alexandria, LA MSA
    686688  3784.0   1461.0    181.5    470.0  Allentown-Bethlehem, PA-NJ MSA
    130542  1361.9    525.8     95.9    248.3  Altoona, PA MSA
    187547  4723.9   1823.9     39.7    102.8  Amarillo, TX MSA
    226338  4396.9   1697.6     51.5    133.3  Anchorage, AK MSA
    130669  1171.1    452.2    111.6    289.0  Anderson, IN MSA
    145196  1859.7    718.0     78.1    202.2  Anderson, SC MSA
    116034  1576.0    608.5     73.6    190.7  Anniston, AL MSA
    315121  3623.1   1398.9     87.0    225.3  Appleton-Oshkosh-Neenah, WI MSA
    174821  1699.8    656.3    102.8    266.4  Asheville, NC MSA
    156267  2417.6    933.4     64.6    167.4  Athens, GA MSA
   2833511 13264.5   5121.5    213.6    553.3  Atlanta, GA MSA
    319416  2114.4    816.4    151.1    391.3  Atlantic City, NJ MSA
    396809  5042.7   1947.0     78.7    203.8  Augusta, GA-SC MSA
    781572  7230.5   2791.7    108.1    280.0  Austin, TX MSA
    543477 21086.8   8141.6     25.8     66.8  Bakersfield, CA MSA
   2382172  6758.0   2609.3    352.5    913.0  Baltimore, MD MSA
     88745   911.2    351.8     97.4    252.2  Bangor, ME MSA
    528264  4109.1   1586.5    128.6    333.0  Baton Rouge, LA MSA
    135982  1836.0    708.9     74.1    191.8  Battle Creek, MI MSA
```

Screenshot from U.S. Census Bureau Web site, American FactFinder (http://factfinder.census.gov), 2009.

Question 12: What is the percent increase in size for each city between 1990 and 2000?

Question 13: What is the change in housing unit density for each city during the same period?

Question 14: Notice that for 1990 data, there is no differentiation between "Water area" and "Land area" for the size of the MSAs. How will this affect the calculation of housing unit density for these two years?

Question 15: Look back at your answer for Question 9. Is the city you selected here also the city with the least increase in housing unit density?

✦ 3.3
Population Density in the City

In the first two exercises, you looked at population density as a relatively simple concept: the distribution of people over space. Even though people are constantly moving around on the earth, it is possible to represent their general locations through population density maps. A map of global population density shows, generally, the distribution of people per country, even though people are moving between those countries.

The problem is that at larger scales (county, city, or neighborhood), mapping the locations of population densities becomes more slippery because the movement of people increasingly becomes a relevant factor to consider.

For example, we can map the population density of Michigan by county, as shown in the map below. The map shows general population density by residence in each county. Because people are continuously traveling between the counties, the map doesn't necessarily show where people actually are during the day. It shows the density if every person was at home, whatever and wherever that home might be. So, the map shows a kind of theoretical density of people that never technically exists.

The larger the scale of the map, the harder it is to find an accurate representation of population density because of human movement.

If the map is based on the U.S. Census, the data "population density" depicts the locations of individual or family dwellings. A census population density map is actually a **dwelling density map** of the city.

So how do we map population density at the city level? Does dwelling density portray an accurate picture of people in the city? Is there a better way to visualize urban population in a map?

Urban geographers have long considered the changing nature of the city depending on the time of day. The day city has different inhabitants, with different activities, than the night city, and the weekend city is different again. These changing dimensions of the city by day and night are central to interpreting urban social structure.

But can the actual shifting locations of individuals themselves be displayed and analyzed with a map?

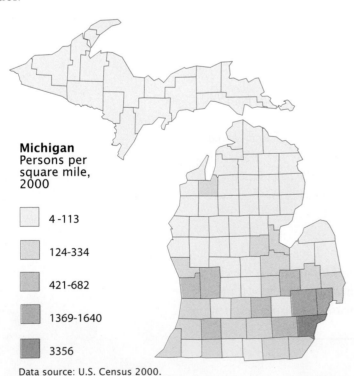

Michigan
Persons per square mile, 2000

- 4 - 113
- 124 - 334
- 421 - 682
- 1369 - 1640
- 3356

Data source: U.S. Census 2000.

This is a question that cartographer Janos Szegö has sought to answer. Szegö looked for a more complex picture of urban population dynamics, one which would go beyond dwelling density. He considered that the average person's life is divided into two broad categories of activity: work and home. How do those spaces compare, and how do they impact the urban infrastructure? To visualize the contrasting densities, he used a particular type of thematic map, the **isarithmic map.**

In this exercise, you will follow Szegö's isarithmic maps to discover a deeper picture of population density in and around the city of Kalamazoo, in southern Michigan. In the steps that follow, you will need a calculator for some simple arithmetic.

The Isarithmic Map

An **isarithmic map** depicts quantitative data as a smooth, continuous surface, using lines to connect numbers of equal value. The numbers of equal value might be point data, for example, surveyed elevation points. The numbers could also be collected by geographic area, as in population numbers collected by state, metro area, or other census division.

One common type of isarithmic map in the United States is the topographical map series of the U.S. Geological Survey (USGS). A USGS "topo" is an isarithmic map because it uses contour lines

to show a continuous surface of elevation data. In Chapter 2, you analyzed an early topographical map from the United Kingdom on pages 14–15, and from the United States on page 19. National weather maps in newspapers also commonly use isarithms to depict rainfall or temperature.

But isarithms can also be used to depict human geographical information. Because they show data as a continuous surface, isarithmic maps are useful for visualizing the volume of flow of people as they move around a city. In the next few maps, we will explore the extent to which isarithmic mapping can help us understand flows of people in Kalamazoo.

Question 1: To get oriented, study the locator map for Kalamazoo, below. Examine the street pattern and landmark information provided in the map. Where would you say downtown is? Where do you think the industrial areas are? What in the map gives you this impression?

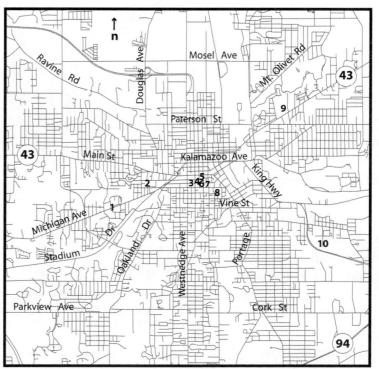

1   University
2   College
3   Art Center
4   Civic Center
5   County
      Courthouse
6   City Hall
7   Library
8   Hospital
9   Medical
      Center
10 County
      Fairgrounds

Base map data source: Michigan Geographic Data Library (www.michigan.gov/cgi).

Question 2: Now that you are somewhat oriented in the city, study the isarithmic maps for the city on the right. In which parts of town is dwelling density highest? Where is it lowest? Where is worker density highest? Lowest? (You can use the landmarks in the locator map to help explain your answer.)

Question 3: How does worker density compare to dweller density? Are there places where both maps show high densities?

Question 4: How does this comparison of dweller and worker densities compare to your impression from the locator map? How has your impression of the city changed?

Question 5: These isarithmic maps show the two major activity fields in a person's day: activity at work and activity at home. What other fields of activity not included here comprise daily urban life?

Dweller density, Kalamazoo 1998

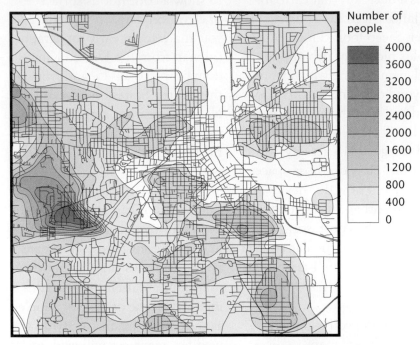

Number of people

4000
3600
3200
2800
2400
2000
1600
1200
800
400
0

Data source: Courtesy of Kalamazoo Area Transportation Study (KATS).
Base map data source: Michigan Geographic Data Library (www.michigan.gov/cgi).

Worker density, Kalamazoo 1998

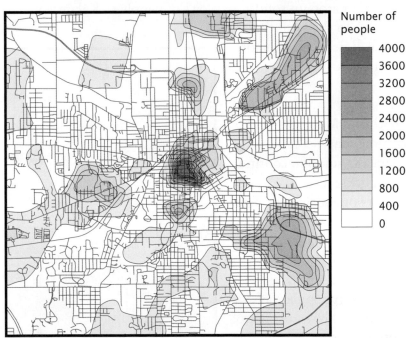

Number of people

4000
3600
3200
2800
2400
2000
1600
1200
800
400
0

Data source: Courtesy of Kalamazoo Area Transportation Study (KATS).
Base map data source: Michigan Geographic Data Library (www.michigan.gov/cgi).

Once we have information about locations of workers and dwellers, we can use the map to extract information about the flow of people in the city. For example, if we assume that people are at their workplaces during the day and at their homes at night, we can make the further assumption that dweller density resembles the city's "nighttime density," and worker density resembles the city's "daytime density." Szegö estimated that, typically, a person spends ten hours a day at work (8 a.m. to 6 p.m.) and fourteen hours a day at home (6 p.m. to 8 a.m.). This information can be used to convert the isarithms in the first map from the "number of people" to the number of "personhours" spent in each space.

Nighttime Personhours, Kalamazoo 1998

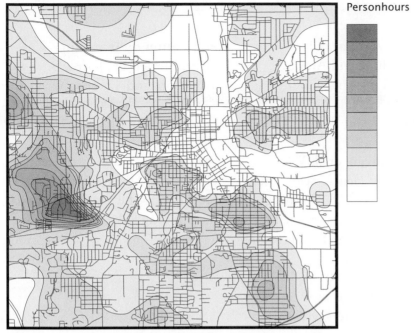

Personhours

Data source: Courtesy of Kalamazoo Area Transportation Study (KATS).
Base map data source: Michigan Geographic Data Library
(www.michigan.gov/cgi).

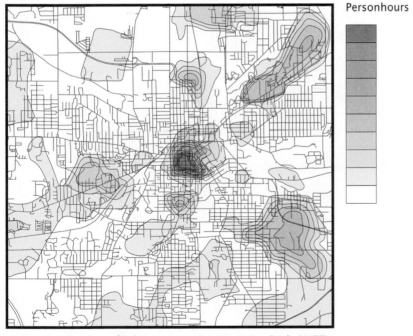

Personhours

Data source: Courtesy of Kalamazoo Area Transportation Study (KATS).
Base map data source: Michigan Geographic Data Library
(www.michigan.gov/cgi).

For the dweller density map, the formula for personhours is:
Number of people × 14.

For the worker density map, the formula for personhours is:
Number of workers × 10.

Question 6: Convert the population density isarithms in the Dweller Density map and the Worker Density map to personhour density isarithms. The isarithms themselves will not change; all you have to do is create new labels for each legend category on the right side of the legend boxes (use photocopies if you are handing in this exercise).

Question 7: Compare your two new personhours maps. How do they compare?

Question 8: Why do you think an urban geographer or planner would be interested in day and night maps of personhours?

Question 9: What are the limitations of using the data to make assumptions about time of day and personhours? (Hint: Think about your answers to Questions 4 and 5.)

To Szegö, understanding where people are in a city is the most fundamental awareness that one can have about how a city works:

What are the networks that create the relationships between the different components of a town? The answer is simply one word: people. It is people and the networks created by their lifelines, spun like webs around buildings, between buildings and squares, from small rooms to lofty galleries, private gardens and parks, that create the invisible structure of a living town. [Szegö, 1994: 218]

Sources and Suggested Readings

Population Indicators

Interactive and Animated Population Periods. http://www.carto.net/papers/svg/sample/pop_pyramids.shtml

Geography of Sprawl

Campoli, Julie and Alex S. Maclean. *Visualizing Density.* Cambridge, Mass.: Lincoln Institute of Land Policy, 2007.

Fulton, William, et al. *Who Sprawls Most? How Growth Patterns Differ Across the U.S.* Washington, D.C.: Center on Urban & Metropolitan Policy, The Brookings Institution, 2001.

Visualizing Density. www.lincoln inst.edu/subcenters/visualizing–density/

Population by Isarithm

Dent, Borden D., Jeffrey S. Torguson, and Thomas W. Hadler. *Cartography: Thematic Map Design.* Sixth ed. N.Y.: McGraw-Hill, 2009.

Szegö, Janos. *Mapping Hidden Dimensions of the Urban Scene.* Stockholm: The Swedish Council for Building Research, 1994.

CHAPTER

4

Language

Vocabulary applied in this chapter
linguistic culture region
core/periphery
language families
habitat
dialect culture region
isoglosses
toponymy
linguistic refuge area

New vocabulary
bivariate map
quantitative data
qualitative data

⊕ ⊕ 4.1
Linguistic Regions and Ecology Online

In this section you will explore some of the concepts of linguistic geography using the language data at the *National Atlas of Canada Online*.

First published in 1906 and produced by the Canadian government, the *National Atlas of Canada* is a regularly updated source for visualizing both the physical and human geography of the country.

For the sixth edition, the atlas ceased to be a paper product and is now operated as an online, interactive atlas. One of the first electronic atlases to be freely available over the Web, this atlas also offers more mapping tools and data layers than most online atlases.

Bilingualism and Linguistic Culture Regions

Both English and French are considered the official languages of Canada, with about 90 percent of the population speaking English or French as their primary language at home according to the 1996 census.

What does Canada's "linguistic duality" look like? Is bilingualism a separate region, or is it simply the relationship between two formal language regions? This exercise looks at the **linguistic culture regions** of the two official languages in detail.

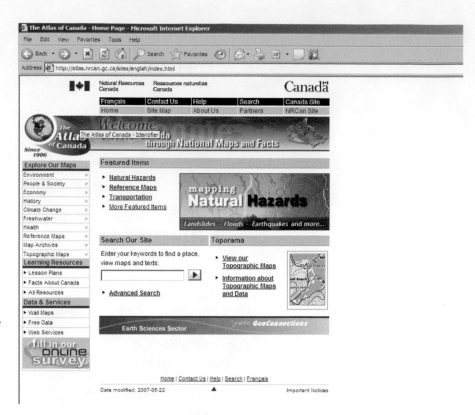

Screenshot from The Atlas of Canada Website at http://atlas.nrcan.gc.ca, © 2009 Her Majesty the Queen in Right of Canada with permission of Natural Resources Canada.

Step 1 Launch your browser and navigate to the "National Atlas of Canada Online" link under Exercise 4.1 in the "Exploring Human Geography with Maps" section of the *Human Mosaic* Web site. This will take you to the main page for the National Atlas of Canada Online, shown above.

Step 2 In the left column, under "Explore Our Maps," choose "People & Society — Languages" and then under the heading "Official Languages, 1996," choose "Knowledge of English, 1996 Map." This will launch your first linguistic map of Canada.

Step 3 Study the map that results. The Legend to the right of the map explains the meaning of the colors and symbols used in the map.

(Notice that for this data set, the data is gathered only at populated areas; places without significant populations, and therefore no census data, are shown in grey.)

To get a closer look at the data set, you can zoom in and out using the zoom magnifying tool buttons on the tool bar above the map.

Question 1: Describe the core/periphery pattern of the formal culture region of English in Canada.

Step 4 Return to the list of available layers in the left column, and choose "People & Society — Languages — Knowledge of French, 1996 Map." This will redraw your map with "Knowledge of French" as the only visible layer.

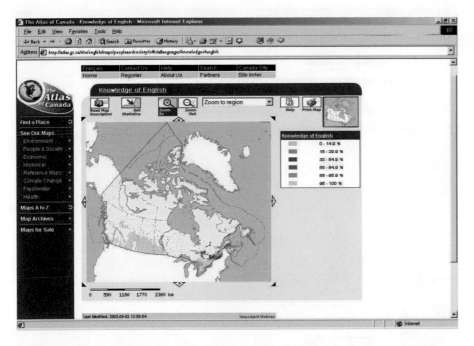

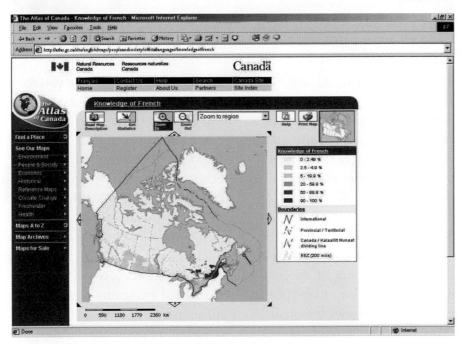

Two screenshots above from The Atlas of Canada Website at http://atlas.nrcan.gc.ca, © 2009 Her Majesty the Queen in Right of Canada with permission of Natural Resources Canada.

Step 5   Now, repeat the process from Step 4 to view the layer "English-French Bilingualism, 1996 Map," and study the results.

Question 3: How is English-French bilingualism regionally distributed?

Question 4: Is there a strong correlation between the core areas of bilingualism and the peripheral areas of French knowledge or English knowledge?

Question 5: Explore the map more closely, considering rural areas versus urban areas. Is there a correlation between the urban or rural character of a place and the level of bilingualism?

Question 6: Is the identity of a populated place as a coastal or inland place a factor in bilingualism? Is proximity to the United States a factor?

Habitat and the Bivariate Map

The Atlas of Canada Online also allows us to look at different data sets simultaneously to see how different linguistic variables are related. This type of data comparison can be used to explore the relationship between **habitat** and language. Although habitat sometimes refers to a wide range of contextual variables influencing language (such as community size and political issues), in this exercise we will explore it as the relationship between language and physical geography.

Because the "Official Languages" data set is symbolized as a choropleth map each time, only one layer of data is visible at a time.

Question 2: Describe the core/ periphery pattern of the formal culture region of French. How is it different from the English culture region?

Step 6   Return to the list of layers in the left column, and select "People & Society — Aboriginal Languages — Aboriginal Languages by Community, 1996." The map that you see should look like the image on the right.

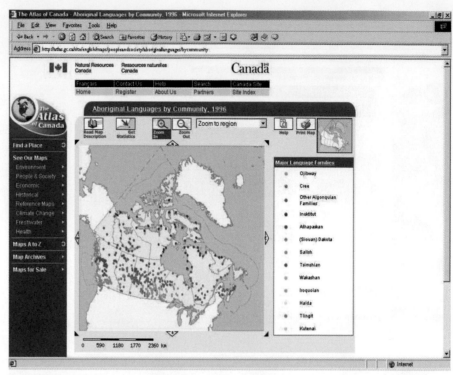

The Atlas of Canada Website http://atlas.nrcan.gc.ca © 2009 Her Majesty the Queen in Right of Canada with permission of Natural Resources Canada.

Question 7: Study the linguistic differences shown in this small-scale map. What region of Canada has the greatest diversity of aboriginal languages? What region has the least diversity?

Question 8: Review the connection between landscape and linguistic diversity that you have learned in class and reading. What would you expect the landscape to be like in the region with the highest density of language families? the lowest density?

Step 7   Zoom in on any region of the map by clicking the "Zoom in" magnifying tool on the tool bar, and clicking your cursor on the map to activate the zoom. You will see that the point symbols show not only the language spoken, but also the number of speakers at that point.

The depiction of two data variables in one map is called a **bivariate map.** Any type of thematic map can be bivariate.

Question 9: Consider the way in which the two data sets are symbolized in this online map. What type of thematic map is this?

The bivariate symbols in this map are combining two major types of data: **quantitative data,** which is ranked or numerical, and **qualitative data,** which is categorically different and therefore cannot be ranked.

The size of the circle shows the quantitative data, in this case— the population size of the community. The color or hue of the point symbol shows the qualitative data, the major language family for that community. Both types of symbols are explained separately in the legend to the right of the map.

Step 8   Explore the aboriginal language geography by panning around the map. Compare some of the communities by clicking the "Get Statistics" button above the map, and clicking on one of

the circles. This will take you to a pop-up window with data for the number of speakers in the community. If you click on the link for "Aboriginal Community Statistics" in the pop-up, you can delve into actual population numbers as well as socioeconomic data for the community.

As you explore, you will notice that there are strong regional differences in language families, community populations, and number of speakers.

Is there a close connection between linguistic regions, number of speakers, and physical geography? In the next section, we will explore this question by zooming in to the region of southern British Columbia and Alberta.

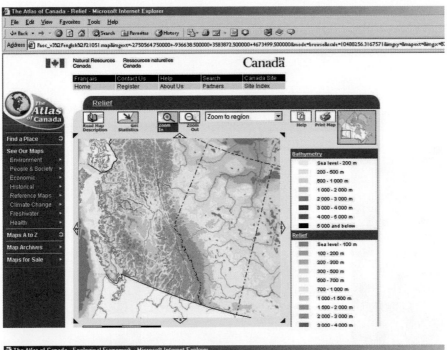

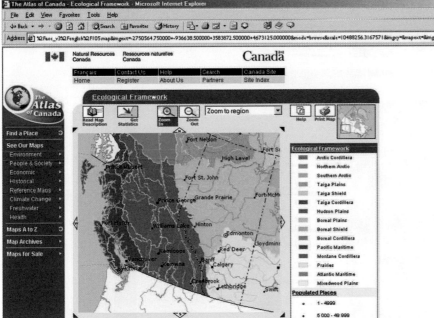

Two screen shots above from The Atlas of Canada Website at http://atlas.nrcan.gc.ca, © 2009 Her Majesty the Queen in Right of Canada with permission of Natural Resources Canada.

Question 10: What are the majority language family or families in use in this region?

Question 11: Compare the geographic information that you see in the linguistic map with the maps of relief and ecological framework, left. Can you find evidence for a linguistic refuge area? Explain your findings.

Step 10   Analyze both the population and number of speakers information in this region by comparing the statistics for the larger communities with the statistics for the smaller communities. Compare your findings to the maps on the left.

Question 12: Is there a relationship between number of speakers and land relief? Between number of speakers and ecological framework?

Question 13: What is the relationship between number of speakers and size of the populated place? Why do you think this is?

Question 14: What seems to be the typical size of the populated place where an aboriginal language family is located?

Although this atlas includes physical mapping layers such as relief and ecological information, these layers cannot be viewed simultaneously. To help you make comparisons, the data layers for Relief and Ecological Framework (from the "Environment—Land" section of the atlas) are provided in the two figures, above.

Step 9   Zoom to the region of Southern British Columbia and Alberta. Explore the map using your pan and zoom tools.

⊕ 4.2
Visualizing Vernacular Dialects

What do the **dialect culture regions** of the United States look like? How does the way we visualize dialect regions in maps affect the way we see these regions? Between 1965 and 1970, the *Dictionary of American Regional English (D.A.R.E.)* project indexed and mapped the vernacular dialect regions of the United States, through field interviews in 1002 communities.

In 1999, linguist Bert Vaux began a new mapping project for the United States, the Dialect Survey, using a public online survey in order to access a national sample of speakers of all ages. The Dialect Survey tracks regional differences in pronunciation, grammar, terminology, and definitions, and displays the results as point data on a map. To address the question of mobility in the speakers' backgrounds, survey respondents identified their locations based on where they consider their primary home place, regardless of their current residence.

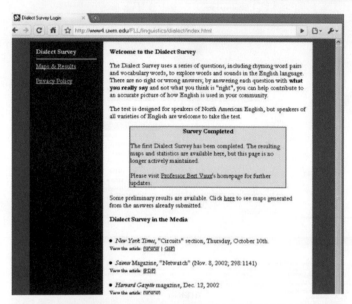

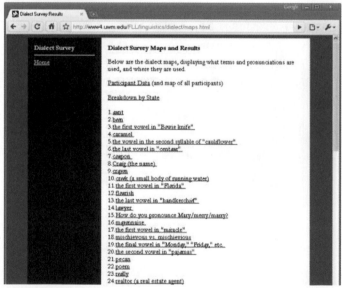

Screenshots courtesy of Bert Vaux, Kings College.

Step 1 Launch your browser and navigate to the "Dialect Survey" link under Exercise 4.2 in the "Exploring Human Geography with Maps" section of the *Human Mosaic* Website. This will take you to the main page for the Dialect Survey, shown here.

Step 2 Click on "Maps & Results" in the upper-left corner.

Step 3 From "Dialect Survey Maps and Results," explore the list of 122 questions you find here, and follow the question links to the mapped results.

Unlike in the dot distribution map in Chapter 7, the dots on these maps represent actual locations of information, that is, the home place for each respondent.

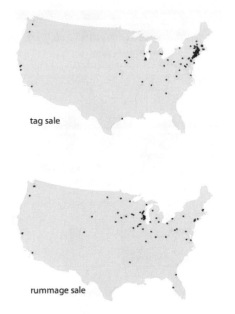

tag sale

sidewalk sale

garage sale

rummage sale

carport sale

stoop sale

Question 1: Choose a word that shows a strong regional differentiation in the maps. How are environmental, industrial, or cultural factors influencing the distribution of dialect in this case?

Question 2: What are some of the words that show little regional differentiation in the maps? Can you speculate about why regional differentiation has been lost for each of these cases?

Step 4   Now turn back to the pages of this workbook. The six maps above display the results for the Dialect Survey question, "Which of these terms do you prefer for a sale of unwanted items on your porch, in your yard, etc.?"

Question 3: Compare the distributions in these maps. What regional differences are evident?

Question 4: What do these terms tell us about changes in the vernacular landscape of the United States?

Although these maps display survey results using point locations of speakers, linguistic geographers have traditionally used **isoglosses** to map dialect. As lines separating areas where particular words and pronunciations are used or not used, isoglosses aggregate individual point locations of speakers into visible dialect culture regions.

Step 5   Make a photocopy of this page. On the copy, draw in the isoglosses for each of the six maps

Question 5: Based on the isogloss map you drew, what is the difference in the dialect distributions you see? What kinds of trends are emphasized? Have any details been lost?

Question 6: Compare your dialect region boundaries to the dialect culture regions map on page 120 in your textbook. Are any similarities evident?

Exploring social differences within dialect regions

One factor influencing dialect geography is the characteristics of the speakers themselves. To what extent do socioeconomic factors also play into word usage, and how do these factors vary when compared across geographical regions?

At the Dialect Topography project, Canadian linguist Jack Chambers designed an English dialect mapping project which tracks, in addition to regions, other factors contributing to dialect useage such as age, class, gender, mobility, language, education, and occupation in the rural and urban areas of southern Ontario and Quebec.

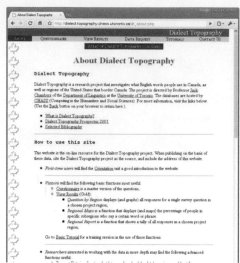
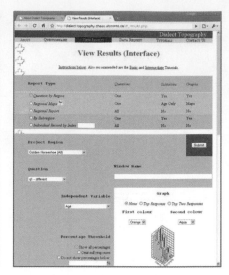

Screenshots, Dialect Topography of Canada © J. K. Chambers 2002. Free interactive database <http://dialect.topography.chass.utoronto.ca>

Step 6   Launch your browser and navigate to the "Dialect Topography" link under Exercise 4.2 in the "Exploring Human Geography with Maps" section of the *Human Mosaic* Website. This will take you to the main page for the Atlas of Dialect Topography, shown above, left.

Step 7   Click "Enter" to proceed to the main page of the site, "About Dialect Topography," as in the screenshot, above center.

Step 8   From the top row of tabs, click on "Questionnaire" to go to the master list of questions from the survey. Without completing the questionnaire, explore the language questions in parts 1 through 5.

Question 7: Which of these questions depends, do you think, on the age of the respondent?

Choose any one of the 76 questions that you find interesting and that seems to be related to age differences, and record the number.

Question 8: From the list of personal questions at the beginning of the questionnaire, which of the other factors do you think also might have an effect on the outcome of your particular mapping question?

Step 9   From the top of the questionnaire page, click the tab "View results" to navigate to the View Results (Interface) page above, right.

Step 10   For "Report Type," click "Regional Maps." For "Project Region," select "Golden Horseshoe (All)." (The Golden Horseshoe is the name of the region of southern Ontario and western New York State that comprises the horseshoe-shaped western section of Lake Ontario.) For "Question," select the question you chose from the questionnaire in Step 8, above. For "Independent Variable," choose "Age." Leave the other radio buttons at their default settings, and hit "Submit Query."

Step 11   In the "Regional Maps" window, the full text of your question is given along with a dropdown menu displaying the various answers from which the respondents chose. For "Variant," choose any one of the variants to map. For "Map Type," choose "Percentages by age." Then hit "Submit Query."

A graph will begin to form, and then a series of choropleth maps will gradually load as well. The maps are in pairs: on the left is a spectral color scheme, and on the right is a map of the same results in a single hue scheme.

Question 9: Interpret the result you see in the maps. For the variant you chose, is age a differentiating factor?

Question 10: Does the answer to that question depend on whether you are looking at the Canadian or United States side of the horseshoe?

Step 12   Return to the "Regional Maps (Interface) – Golden Horseshoe" window (Step 11, above) and map the other variants of your question.

Question 11: Which of your variants is associated with younger respondents, and which variant is associated with older respondents?

Step 13   Now return to the "View Results (Interface)" page (Step 10). This time, for "Independent Variable," choose "Sex." For "Report Type," choose "Question by Region." Then, hit "Submit Query." A new window called "DT Results" will load, with a table of question variants with the responses tabulated by male and female.

Question 12: Does gender appear to be a factor in the way that people responded to this question? What are the differences?

Step 14   On the DT Results, scroll down to the purple table for "Regional Comparison," as in the screenshot below. Choose any two regions to see how your chosen question varies by sex in those places, and hit "Submit."

Question 13: Does geographical region appear to be a factor in the way that people responded to this question; if so, how?

Question 14: What can you now conclude about gender, age, and region for your particular dialect question?

Question 15: Throughout this exercise, you have mapped dialect geography by point locations, isoglosses, and choropleth maps. Which mapping technique, in your opinion, is best suited to visualizing vernacular dialect, and why is it more effective than the others?

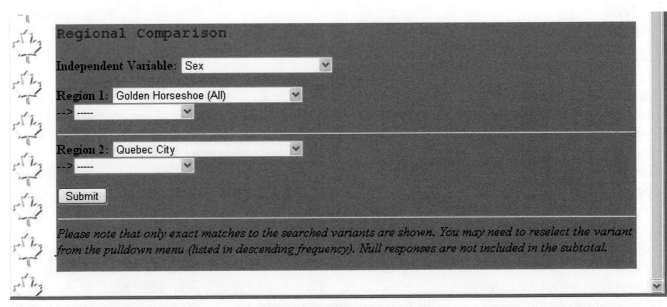

Screenshot, Dialect Topography of Canada © J. K. Chambers 2002. Free interactive database <http://dialect.topography.chass.utoronto.ca>

"New England," by John Smith. In *A description of New-England: or The observations and discoueries, of Captain Iohn Smith....* London 1616. Collection of the William L. Clements Library, University of Michigan. Used with permission.

● 4.3
The Power of Place Names

Maps can powerfully shape our cultural worldviews. Part of that power stems from the place names associated with particular geographic features, also called **toponymy.** The language of place names, the familiarity or unfamiliarity of their sound and spelling, and even the number and density of named features all contribute to the way in which we perceive the geography of a place.

What do place names on a map tell us about the languages actively spoken in a particular place? Sometimes, very little. Much of cartography stems from the outside looking in, and may as much portray the linguistic hopes or ambitions of the map-maker as the linguistic reality of the place in the map.

In fact, maps are so useful for replacing one culture's toponymy with another, that they have been put to use as traditional tools for the colonization and domination of populations.

For example, consider the 1616 map by John Smith, above. Smith used this map to depict the northeastern region of North America, the theater of his northern explorations, for European audiences. At that time, the region was wholly an indigenous landscape, shaped, cultivated, named, and mapped by native people. The map, however, portrays a land filled with English toponyms, though the first English colonists would not begin arriving at Plymouth for another four years. On this map, Smith notes that the Prince of Wales provided the place names.

Question 1: Why do you think Smith would depict the region in this way, knowing that there was yet no English settlement in the area?

Question 2: What do you think are the long-term effects of removing indigenous place names during colonization?

Today, returning Indigenous place names to the map is a priority in places around the world that are undergoing decolonization, or where there is active resistance to colonization.

In Mexico, Guatemala, Wales, Ireland, Canada, and the United States, cultures that have been linguistically colonized are now adding or replacing their own toponyms on maps depicting their territory. By remapping the Indigenous words, they are reclaiming their linguistic imprint, and thus their cultural imprint, on the land.

One person who is working to preserve place names through mapping is the Irish cartographer Tim Robinson. Robinson began walking and exploring the Aran Islands on the western coast of Ireland in 1972.

The only available map of the islands at that time was a relic of the British Ordnance Survey mapping of Ireland during the nineteenth century. In that survey, British surveyors set down Irish toponymy with anglicized words that sounded similar to the original Irish word, creating new, colonized, toponymic landscapes on the maps.

Disappointed in the place names provided on his Ordnance Survey map, Robinson set out to remap the original Irish names in the landscape himself, by walking and asking questions of people he met along the way.

He began with the Island of Árainn, and the result, part of which is shown on page 54, is a map and text brimming with Irish place names and stories never before set down in print. In his map, numbers refer to stories and additional place names described in a supplementary text.

Robinson's map differs greatly from the early OSI (Ordnance Survey of Ireland) map of this area, shown on page 55. The top map also depicts the southeast section of the Island of Árainn. The two images below it are close-ups from two sections of the map, to give you an idea of the place name geography.

Question 3: Compare the nature and distribution of the place names in the OSI map with those in Robinson's map. In what ways do they differ? Are there any similarities?

Question 4: Assuming that you have not traveled to Árainn, what kind of mental picture of this place do you form from the OSI map? What would you expect the physical landscape to be like? What would you expect of the cultural landscape?

Question 5: Does the Robinson map give you the same picture? Why or why not?

Question 6: In what way is physical landscape connected to the life of a language? Do mapmakers play a role in this connection?

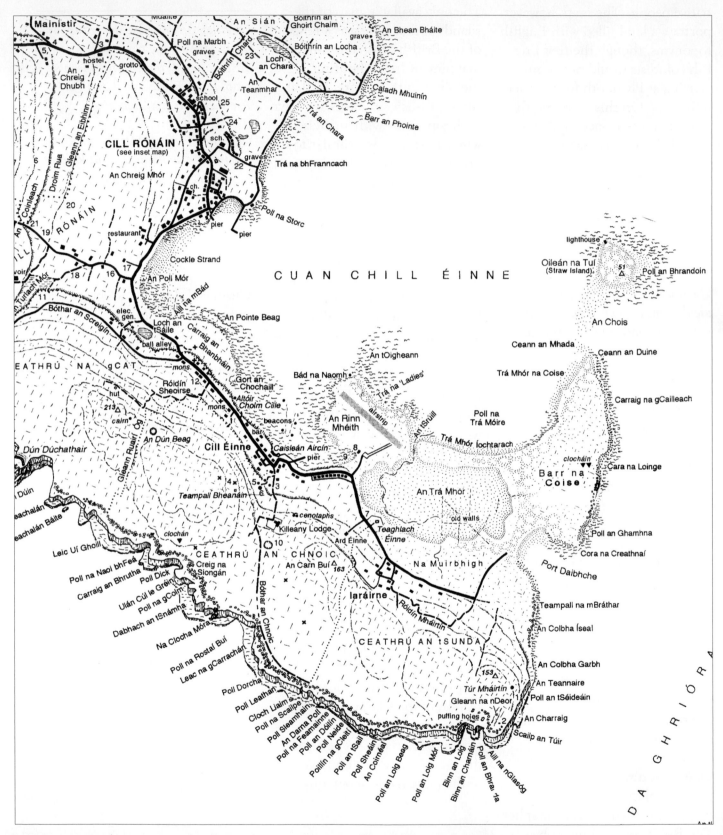

Detail from "Oileáin Árann" by Tim Robinson, © 1996 Folding Landscapes. Used with permission of the author and publisher.

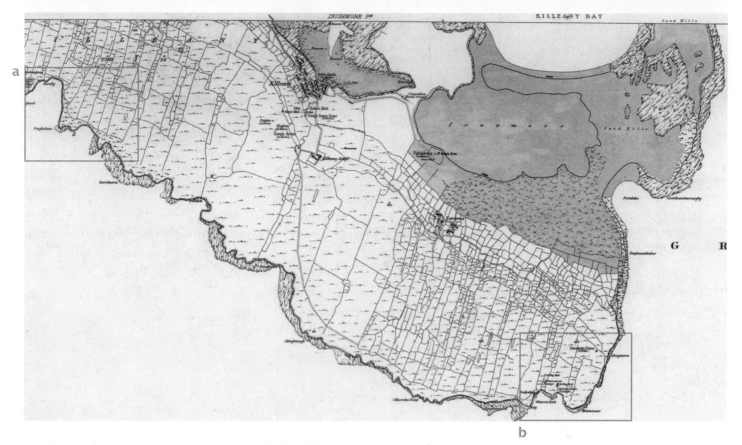

a

b

a

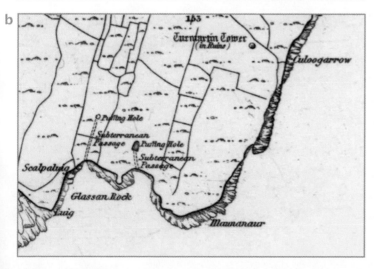

b

Details above and left from "County Galway Sheet 119," British Ordnance Survey of Ireland, 1901. Courtesy of the Geography and Map Division, Library of Congress.

Sources and Suggested Readings

Multivariate Explorations

Monmonier, Mark. *Mapping It Out: Expository Cartography for the Humanities and Social Sciences.* Chicago: University of Chicago Press, 1993.

Monmonier, Mark. *How to Lie with Maps.* Chicago: University of Chicago Press, 1991.

Locating Vernacular Dialect

Cassidy, Frederic G., ed. *Dictionary of American Regional English.* 3 vols. Cambridge, Mass.: Harvard University Press, 1985–2002.

Irish Place Names

Robinson, Tim. "Oileáin Árainn." [map] 1:28,160. Roundstone, Ireland: Folding Landscapes, 1996.

Robinson, Tim. *Setting Foot on the Shores of Connemara & Other Writings.* Dublin: Lilliput Press, 1996.

CHAPTER
5

Ethnicity

Vocabulary applied in this chapter
ethnic group
ethnic homeland
ethnic island
ethnic neighborhood

New vocabulary
enumeration unit
percentiles
classification scheme
census tract
equal intervals classification
  scheme
percentiles scheme
class breaks
class width
outliers

⊕ 5.1
Census Tools for Mapping Ethnic Diversity

In Exercise 3.2, you used an online mapping tool of the U.S. Census, American FactFinder, to explore some basic population numbers in two cities. In this exercise, we will return to more fully explore the data and tools freely available at this Web site while increasing our understanding of the geography of ethnicity across the United States.

Step 1 Launch your Web browser, and navigate to the "American Factfinder" link under Exercise 5.1 in the "Exploring Human Geography with Maps" section of the *Human Mosaic* Web site. This will take you to the main page for American FactFinder, shown here.

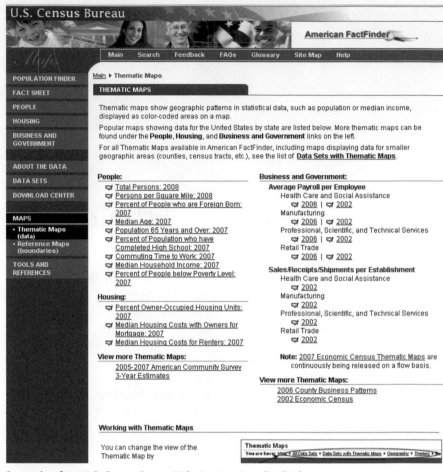

Screenshot from U.S. Census Bureau Web site, American FactFinder (http://factfinder.census.gov), 2009.

FactFinder allows you to explore a myriad of socioeconomic data by tables, maps, or both. Occupation, number of foster children in the family, travel time to work, and language spoken at home, are just some of the variables accessible here. Which particular data is available depends on the geographic scale that you are viewing (for example, state, county, or metropolitan areas) and whether the type of display you would like to view is a table or a map.

For this exercise, we will focus on the mapping function to help visualize spatial differences in **ethnic groups.**

Step 2   Click on "Maps" in the left column and select "Thematic Maps (data)." Under the "People" heading, choose "Persons per Square Mile: 2008." You are now at the main mapping page of FactFinder.

To get to the ethnicity data, you first need to change the data set displayed in the map. Notice in the upper-left corner of the Web page, there is a line that begins "You are here" and displays the path that resulted in your map of population density. FactFinder allows you to browse a number of different census data sets. Each data set shows different kinds of population information.

Step 3   From the "You are here" menu bar in the left corner of the screen, select the "Data Sets with Thematic Maps" step in the path. Doing so will take

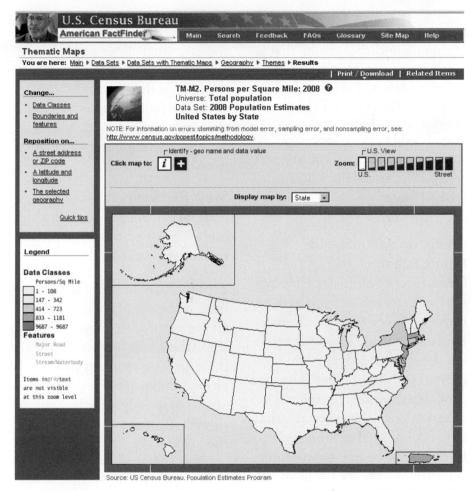

U.S. Census Bureau Web site. Census 2000, Summary File 1. American FactFinder (http://factfinder.census.gov), 2009.

you to a list of data sets available for mapping. You can get a list of themes within each data set by selecting one and clicking on the "What's This?" button.

For this exercise, we want to look at the ancestry themes, which are in the data set "Census 2000 Summary File 3 (SF 3)–Sample Data."

Step 4   Choose "Census 2000 Summary File 3 (SF 3)– Sample Data" and click the "Next" button.

Next you need to specify where in the United States you would like to view this data. We'll start with the country as a whole.

Step 5   From the "Select Geography" Web page, leave the selection method at its default of "list." For geographic type, select "Nation." For geographic area, select "United States," then click the "Next" button. You should now be at the "Select Theme" Web page.

Step 6   Choose "by subject" as the theme selection method and go to the "Population Totals–Race and Ethnic Groups" subject category. Choose "Ancestry" and click "Search." The search will return a list of all available ancestry themes to portray in the map.

Step 7 Scroll through the list of themes and choose one that is most interesting to you. When you have selected it from the list, click the "Show Result" button.

You should now be looking at the distribution of the ancestry group by state for the whole United States.

Ethnic Homelands and Ethnic Islands

One aspect of ethnic geography that we can explore from here is the existence of **ethnic homelands** and **ethnic islands.** Examine the generalized map you have created with FactFinder. The map probably shows some regional differentiations, but because the data is presented at the state level, it is not a very good source for analyzing the locations of ethnic homelands and islands. For better detail, you want to change the **enumeration unit** from states to counties.

"Enumeration unit" is a term used to describe the geographic unit (such as county, zip code, or census tract) at which data has been collected.

Step 8 Centered just above the map you will see a menu indicating that you have chosen to "Display map by: State." From the pull-down arrow, change the selection to "County" and wait for the map to redraw.

Step 9 Begin exploring the map for evidence of an ethnic homeland or ethnic islands for this ancestry group.

Tips for exploring: If the black lines of the county boundaries are interfering, try zooming in using the Zoom buttons above the map. You can then pan around the map using the pan arrows at the edges of the map or with the tool available above the map.

If the roads or water features are also interfering, you can turn off these features by going to the left side of the page, above the Legend, and clicking on "Change... Boundaries and features." Select the "Features" tab and turn off the features you don't want, and press "Update" in the upper-right corner.

To identify a particular county, click on the Identify tool, symbolized by the letter "i," and then click on the county you want to identify.

Step 10 Analyze the spatial pattern that you observe in the map.

Question 1: Which ancestry group did you choose? Does this population appear to have an ethnic homeland? If so, describe its location. If you don't think there is an ethnic homeland evident, what characteristic about the spatial pattern in the map gives you that impression?

Question 2: Where are the ethnic islands for this ancestry group? Describe their size and whether they appear to be associated with urban or rural regions.

Close-up on Florida

In this next exercise, we will focus on ethnic patterns in Florida using FactFinder to explore differences in spatial distributions.

Step 11 Using the Zoom and Pan tools, center your map over Florida. If you have not done so already, display the map by counties so that you have a more fine-grained view of the state. You can do this by clicking on the "Display map by: ..." drop-down arrow and selecting "Counties."

Step 12 In order to change the ancestry group to Greek Americans choose "Themes" from the "You are here:" pathway and select the "by subject" tab. As you did in Step 6, choose the "Population Totals-Race and Ethnic Groups" subject category, select "Ancestry," and click "Search." From the list of available ancestries, choose "Percent of Persons of Greek Ancestry: 2000" and then "Show Result."

Question 3: Describe the spatial distribution that you see for Greek ancestry. Where are the ethnic islands located?

Step 13 Continue to explore the ancestry distribution by creating and interpreting maps for three additional ancestry categories: West Indian Ancestry, Italian Ancestry, and United States Ancestry. To change the ancestry theme, follow the instructions in Step 12.

Step 14 Analyze the spatial patterns for West Indian, Italian, and United States ancestries.

Tips for analyzing the spatial patterns: When making comparisons between groups, be sure to take into account the different proportions of each ancestry group.

Notice that the themes are classified differently in each map; for example, dark green may represent 2 percent of the population in one map and 40 percent of the population in another.

If it helps remind you of the distributions, you can print a copy of each map using the "Print / Download" menu from the blue toolbar in the upper-right corner of the page.

Also, if the map is too crowded to read, you can turn map features on or off to assist with your interpretation.

Question 4: How do the spatial patterns of these next three ancestry groups compare to the first? In what ways are they different or the same?

✦ ⊕ 5.2
Hiding and Finding Ethnic Neighborhoods with the Choropleth

Each of the maps you created in Exercise 5.1 is a choropleth map. As you learned in Chapter 3, a **choropleth map** symbolizes data over an area using a color or pattern. The choropleth is a popular mapping tool because it is simple to construct digitally and easy for general audiences to read. Choropleths are ideally suited to mapping data aggregated by enumeration unit (such as county, zip code, or census tract). As a result, it is often the map chosen by geographers to show population characteristics such as income, age, gender, and ethnicity.

Throughout this workbook, we will be using the choropleth map more than any other map. This is not because the choropleth is the best thematic map for human geography. Rather, it reflects the state of technology because the choropleth is easier to automate than other thematic map types. With rare exceptions, Web map applications overwhelmingly use the choropleth map over all other thematic map types.

A choropleth map assigns one color to an area, as if that area were actually a point. Only one data value can be portrayed in a simple choropleth map because one color is assigned to one value. For example, in the ancestry maps you created with Fact-Finder, you could view only one ancestry theme at a time.

If the data to be mapped is one of many different variables, the result is that the choropleth hides as much data as it shows, which can mislead the reader into thinking that there is only one variable.

For instance, if you want to make a map showing the dominant ethnicity for each **ethnic neighborhood** in your city, you would assign one color per neighborhood depending on which group is dominant. All other ethnic groups are hidden.

Would such a map give an accurate portrayal of ethnic diversity? How would you portray the second most dominant ethnic group? For a map of ethnic diversity, the choropleth hides more information than it displays.

What is the solution?

Cartographer Eugene Turner pondered this problem of the hidden data of the choropleth in 1989 while searching for an accurate portrayal of ethnic diversity in Los Angeles. His solution was to make three separate maps of the city, shown on this page.

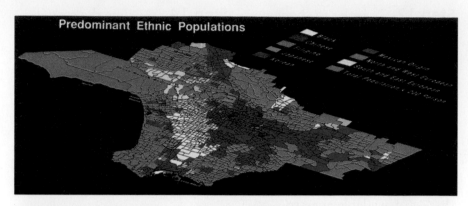

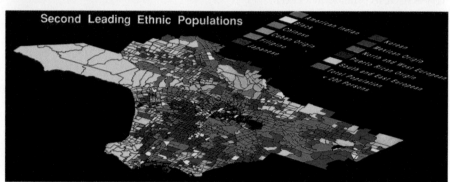

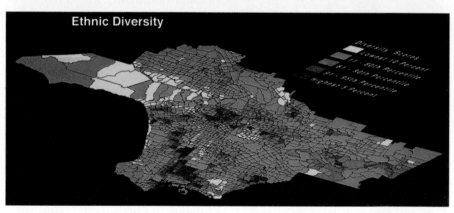

"Leading Ethnicity" (top), "Second Leading Ethnicity" (middle), and "Ethnic Diversity" (bottom), © 1989 Dr. Eugene Turner, California State University, Northridge. Used with permission of the author.

Question 1: Study the three Los Angeles maps. Why did Turner choose these particular categories for his map series?

In the 1990s, Bruce Macdonald pondered this same problem while working on his book, *Vancouver: A Visual History*. Macdonald wanted to accurately portray the character of ethnic neighborhoods in Vancouver. He experimented with the technique of using the area symbolism of the choropleth map to indicate the largest concentration of an ethnic group for each neighborhood. Then for each choropleth area he provided both the percentage of the dominant group for that neighborhood as well as the citywide percentage of that group.

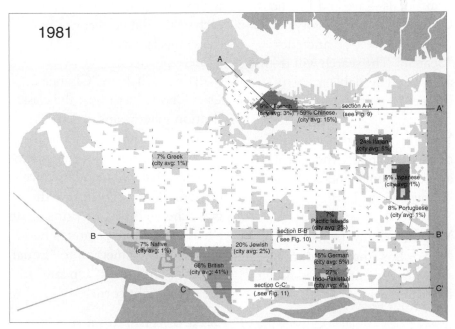

1981

Above: "Largest Ethnic Origin Group by Census Tract, 1981," and right: "Ethnic Cross-Sections" by Bruce Macdonald, from *Vancouver: A Visual History*, Vancouver: Talonbooks © 1992. Used with permission of author and publisher.

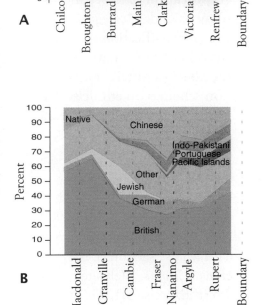

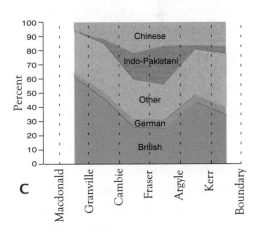

This is illustrated in his map of ethnicity in 1981, above.

This technique allowed him to show whether an ethnic group represented a strong majority in a given neighborhood, or merely the greatest proportion in a neighborhood in which no ethnic group held a majority.

To this altered choropleth Macdonald added three transects of race in his city (the paths labeled A, B, and C in the map), to show the changing ethnic neighborhoods as one travels down the individual streets. These transects are shown to the right of the map.

Question 2: Compare the differences in ethnic neighborhoods as shown by the three transects.

Question 3: How do these transects change your perception of Vancouver's ethnic neighborhoods from the perception given by the altered choropleth map?

Question 4: How does Macdonald's portrayal of ethnic diversity compare with Turner's maps? Which do you think is a more effective solution?

Classification Scheme and Its Effect on Small Details

There are other ways to hide data in a choropleth map.

One way to hide data is to alter the way data values are grouped into categories, called the **classification scheme,** and the number of data categories used in that classification scheme. In this last section, we will explore the effect of different classification schemes on ethnicity data using the tools of FactFinder.

Step 1   Launch your Web browser and navigate to the "American FactFinder" link under Exercise 5.2 in the "Exploring Human Geography with Maps" section of the *Human Mosaic* Web site, as you did in Exercise 5.1. This time, go directly to the data by choosing the highlighted "Data Sets with Thematic Maps" link near the center of the page.

Step 2   Select the "Census 2000 Summary File 3 (SF 3)– Sample Data" data set from the list and press "Next."

Step 3   From the "Select Geography" Web page, leave the selection method at its default of "list." For geographic type, select "Metropolitan Statistical Area / Consolidated Metropolitan Statistical Area." For geographic area select "Los Angeles-Riverside-Orange County, CA CMSA," then click the "Next" button, which will take you to the "Select Theme" Web page.

Step 4   Choose the "by subject" tab as the theme selection method and go to the "Population Totals–Race and Ethnic Groups" subject category, choose "Ancestry," and click "Search." The search will return a list of all available ancestry themes to portray in the map.

Step 5   Scroll through the list of themes, choose the Russian ancestry theme, and click the "Show Result" button.

You should now be looking at a map of Los Angeles County showing Percent of Persons with Russian Ancestry: 2000.

For this exercise, we will explore the data at the level of census tract for the enumeration unit. In U.S. Census data, a **census tract** is an enumeration unit smaller than the county level, averaging about 4,000 people in size.

Step 6   Change the enumeration unit to Census Tract using the "Display map by:" drop-down menu above the map view window.

Now that the enumeration unit is set, what should the classification scheme be? One of the most popular schemes is **equal interval** classification because it is easy to construct. In equal interval classification, the data values in the data set are divided into categories (called "classes") of equal numerical value.

The values which begin and end each of the data categories are

called the **class breaks.** The differences from the highest value to the lowest is called the **class width.** In equal interval schemes, each of the data categories has the same class width.

Step 7   Click on "Change ... Data Classes" to adjust the classification scheme and color palette. Set the number of classes to five intervals and the color scheme to a palette that will print effectively on your printer. **Hint:** Use the gray scheme if you are printing on a black-and-white printer. Then set the classing method to "Equal Interval," and press "Update" in the upper-right corner.

Step 8   Print this map with a legend and then quit FactFinder.

Question 5: Analyze the map you printed. What, in general, is your perception of the geography of Russian Ancestry in Los Angeles County?

Question 6: What are the changes like between census tracts? Is there a smooth or abrupt change in percent ethnicity?

Question 7: Do you think equal intervals are a useful way to categorize Russian Ancestry? Why or why not?

In their atlas of ethnicity and socioeconomic status in Southern California, *The Ethnic Quilt,* James P. Allen and Eugene Turner mapped the spatial distribution of more than 30 individual ethnic identities. To achieve this, the maps in their atlas show

Figure 3.5
Russian Ancestry
Percent of Population
1990

Number of Tracts		Percent Russian
1269		0 - 0.5
795		0.6 - 2.0
241		2.1 - 4.1
129		4.2 - 8.1
107		8.2 - 15.0
5		15.1 - 37.2

County Boundary
City Boundary

Russian
196,467 Persons
42 Median Age
$51,000 Median Household Income
$29,000 Median Personal Income of the US-born
$14,900 Median Personal Income of the foreign-born
13.3 Percent of persons 25 yrs+ who are foreign-born
23.2 Percent of foreign-born persons 25 yrs+ who immigrated 1980-90
94.8 Percent of persons 18 yrs+ who speak English only or very well
45.6 Percent of persons 25 yrs+ who are four-year college graduates
51.3 Percent of employed in managerial and professional occupations
62.5 Percent of occupied homes which are occupied by owner

20 Miles

Statistics and percents are for the Los Angeles CMSA (Los Angeles, Orange, Riverside, San Bernardino and Ventura Counties), 1990.

Figure 5.11
Indonesian
Percent of Population
1990

Number of Tracts		Percent Indonesian
2362		0 - 0.3
114		0.4 - 0.5
58		0.6 - 1.0
30		1.1 - 3.3

County Boundary
City Boundary

Indonesian
10,913 Persons
29 Median Age
$32,000 Median Household Income
$16,554 Median Personal Income of the US-born
$18,000 Median Personal Income of the foreign-born
95.4 Percent of persons 25 yrs+ who are foreign-born
45.4 Percent of foreign-born persons 25 yrs+ who immigrated 1980-90
59.7 Percent of persons 18 yrs+ who speak English only or very well
33.0 Percent of persons 25 yrs+ who are four-year college graduates
27.3 Percent of employed in managerial and professional occupations
53.6 Percent of occupied homes which are occupied by owner

20 Miles

Statistics and percents are for the Los Angeles CMSA (Los Angeles, Orange, Riverside, San Bernardino and Ventura Counties), 1990.

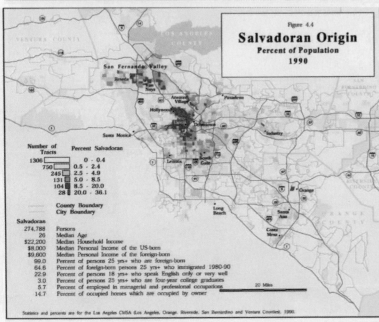

Figure 4.4
Salvadoran Origin
Percent of Population
1990

Number of Tracts		Percent Salvadoran
1306		0 - 0.4
750		0.5 - 2.4
245		2.5 - 4.9
131		5.0 - 8.5
104		8.5 - 20.0
28		20.0 - 36.1

County Boundary
City Boundary

Salvadoran
274,788 Persons
26 Median Age
$22,200 Median Household Income
$8,000 Median Personal Income of the US-born
$9,600 Median Personal Income of the foreign-born
99.0 Percent of persons 25 yrs+ who are foreign-born
64.6 Percent of foreign-born persons 25 yrs+ who immigrated 1980-90
22.9 Percent of persons 18 yrs+ who speak English only or very well
3.0 Percent of persons 25 yrs+ who are four-year college graduates
5.7 Percent of employed in managerial and professional occupations
14.7 Percent of occupied homes which are occupied by owner

20 Miles

Statistics and percents are for the Los Angeles CMSA (Los Angeles, Orange, Riverside, San Bernardino and Ventura Counties), 1990.

the spatial distribution of a single ethnicity as a choropleth map, at the census tract level, using another type of classification: **the percentiles scheme.**

Percentiles allowed Allen and Turner to highlight the **outliers**, the extreme high and low values of the data set, choosing either the bottom 10th or 20th percentile, and adding the top 80th, 90th, and 95th percentiles.

Question 8: Study the Russian Ancestry map by Allen and Turner, and compare it to your equal intervals Russian Ancestry map. Both maps show the same data theme. How are they different?

Question 9: Which classification scheme do you think best represents Russian Ancestry in this case, equal intervals or percentiles? Why?

Question 10: Now compare the three maps by Allen and Turner. How do the percentiles of the three ethnic groups compare?

Question 11: In addition to the choropleth, what technique do they use to give the reader an indication of the total distribution of the data set?

Question 12: Is one of the maps a more effective portrayal of the spatial distribution of the outliers, or do all three effectively portray outliers equally? Explain your interpretation.

"Map Describing the Scituation of the Several Nations of Indians to the N.W. of S. Carolina," British Library Ms 4723. Used with permission of the British Library.

❂ 5.3
Ethnic Diversity as Cultural Perception

The extent to which a map reflects the ethnic diversity of a region depends on many factors. Diversity in the map depends on who the mapmaker chooses to portray in the map, and the message that the mapmaker hopes to convey to the reader.

Diversity in a map also reflects the mapmaker's perceptions or familiarity with the people in the region. Often, our ability to perceive ethnic diversity depends on how familiar we are with a place; we tend to perceive more ethnic diversity among people whom we know, and less diversity among people whom we don't know. Strange or distant populations often fall into broader categories, or under the anonymous category of "Other," or may not be shown at all. By comparing maps of the same region made by different mapmakers, we can explore changes in how cultures perceive the ethnic diversity around them.

The map to the left is an English copy of a Native map drawn on deerskin about 1721 by an unknown person, as a gift to the new governor of South Carolina, Francis Nicholson. The map delineates Nicholson's new territory for him, showing the connections of the Indian nations in relationship to the southern English colonies.

At the heart of these connected nations was a confederacy of 13 distinct cultures having separate languages and customs, dominated by the Nasaws. They maintained social and political ties with their neighbors, the Cherokees and Chickasaws, though these latter nations were not part of the confederacy. The English, on the other hand, perceived these separate nations as a single ethnic identity, known as the Catawbas.

The Native map is drawn in traditional southeastern native cartographic style, using circles to depict Native communities and squares to depict European communities. Charleston is represented as a grid of streets on the left side of the map.

Connecting the circles and squares are double line connections. Running horizontally through the map is a prominent double line connecting Nasaw to Charleston; this line is labeled "The English Path to Nasaw." Scholars have speculated that the lines represent both rivers and paths between native peoples, as well as social and political connections.

As you study the map, you will see that the tribes are symbolized by different circle sizes. Curious about the meaning of the different sizes, anthropologist Gregory Waselkov compared the content of the map to population records from the colonial period, to see whether the circles were similar to the Western technique of using proportional symbols to show population data. He found that there was some correlation between Native populations and circle sizes, but not for all of the circles.

Question 1: What other factors besides population size do you think might influence the circle sizes showing the different nations?

Question 2: What do you think were the motivations of the Native author or authors for portraying this level of cultural complexity in a map for a new colonial governor?

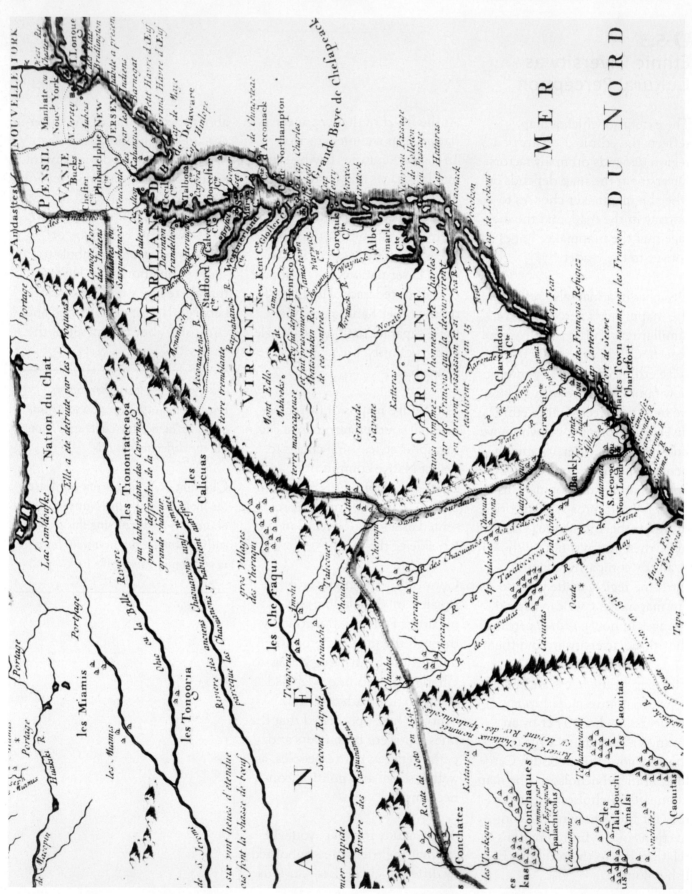

A second map of the southeastern region shows a very different view of diversity in the region. The map on the left is from the French royal geographer Guillaume de l'Isle and depicts the colony of Carolina in 1718. At that time, the French and English were competing with each other for both territorial claims and Indian allegiances in the Southeast.

Study the place name details in de l'Isle's map. To get oriented, Charleston, South Carolina, is shown as "CharlesTown" on the map; it is on the coast in the lower-right-hand corner of the map.

Question 3: Compare the de l'Isle map to the "Catawba" map on page 66. How do the two maps compare in terms of the way that they depict the English colonial claims?

Question 4: How do the two maps differ in the symbols used to differentiate Indian nations? How do they differ in their portrayal of Native towns?

Question 5: For whom do you think de l'Isle's map was created? How do you think this influenced his portrayal of ethnicity in the map?

Sources and Suggested Readings

Mapping Ethnic Diversity

Allen, James P., and Eugene Turner. *The Ethnic Quilt: Population Diversity in Southern California*. Northridge, Calif.: Center for Geographical Studies, 1997.

Brewer, Cynthia A., and Trudy A. Suchan, U.S. Census Bureau, Census Special Reports, Series CENSR/01-1. *Mapping Census 2000: The Geography of U.S. Diversity*. Washington, D.C.: Government Printing Office, 2001.

MacDonald, Bruce. *Vancouver: A Visual History*. Vancouver: Talonbooks, 1994.

Robinson, Arthur. *Early Thematic Mapping in the History of Cartography*. Chicago: University of Chicago Press, 1982.

Ethnic Neighborhoods and the Choropleth Map

MacEachren, Alan M. *Some Truth with Maps: A Primer on Symbolization & Design*. Washington, D.C.: Association of American Geographers, 1994.

Monmonier, Mark. *How to Lie with Maps*. Chicago: University of Chicago Press, 1991.

Cultural Perception in the Southeast

Cumming, William P. *The Southeast in Early Maps*. Chapel Hill: University of North Carolina Press, 1962.

Merrell, James H. *The Indians' New World: Catawbas and Their Neighbors from European Contact through the Era of Removal*. Chapel Hill: University of North Carolina Press, 1989.

Warhus, Mark. *Another America*. N.Y.: St. Martin's Press, 1997.

Waselkov, Gregory A. "Indian Maps of the Colonial Southeast," in Peter H. Wood, Gregory A. Waselkov, and M. Thomas Hartley, eds. *Powhatan's Mantle*. Lincoln: University of Nebraska Press, pp. 292–343.

CHAPTER

6

Politics

Vocabulary applied in this chapter
political landscape
redistricting
electoral regions
gerrymandering
block group
types of boundaries:
  natural, ethnographic,
  geometric, relic

New vocabulary
parallels
meridians
graticule and its properties
map projection types:
  cylindrical, azimuthal/
  planar, conic
Mercator projection
Peters Projection
Winkel Tripel Projection
generalization

⊕ 6.1
The Politics of Projections

The decision about whose political worldview will be represented in a map has inspired some of the most heated debates in geography and politics. Of these debates, perhaps the most contentious is the question of which map projection is the best for showing the countries of the world. This seemingly simple task of choosing a projection that shows all countries with the minimum of distortion has been one of the most difficult and divisive challenges for political geographers and cartographers to solve.

Why is this such a difficult task to accomplish? One reason has to do with the way that lines of latitude (**parallels**)

and lines of longitude (**meridians**)

are arranged when they are removed from the spherical earth.

On the globe, parallels and meridians form a tidy grid called the **graticule:**

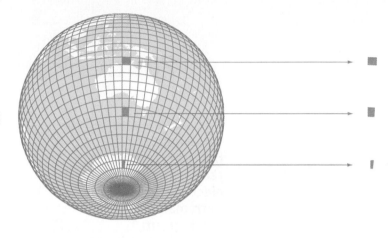

Parallels form concentric circles along the surface of the globe. Meridians, on the other hand, converge gradually toward a point at each pole. The resulting cells of the graticule vary in shape and size, depending on where they fall on the globe. In other words, the cells of the grid on the round globe don't resemble the cells of a grid on flat paper. Before a graticule is flattened, the individual cells already have different sizes and shapes.

Flattening these round cells requires a considerable amount of readjustment to the shapes and sizes of its quadrilaterals. One small readjustment to the graticule will create distortion in the way that the outlines of countries are depicted on the earth. As the graticule is progressively flattened out, these distortions mul-

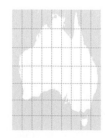

tiply. This arrangement and flattening of the graticule is a **map projection.**

To control the way that a map projection distorts the earth, the cartographer decides which properties of the graticule are the most important to preserve. These properties are: area, distance, direction, and shape. Is the area of a country the most important factor to preserve? If so, then distance and shape are going to suffer. If shape is the most important factor, then the areas of the countries will be distorted.

All properties cannot be preserved in a map projection; some part of the properties of the graticule have to be sacrificed. Which properties are preserved depends on the way in which the graticule is "peeled" from the globe. In general, there are three ways to peel and project the graticule.

A cylindrical projection is created by projecting the graticule onto a plane wrapped around the globe in a cylinder:

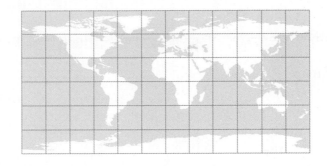

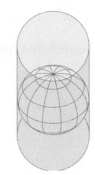

An azimuthal or planar projection is created by projecting the graticule from a point on the globe onto a flat plane:

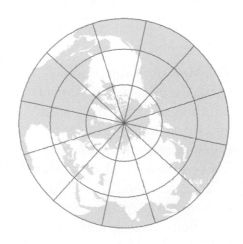

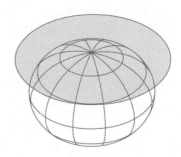

A conic projection is created by projecting the graticule onto a plane wrapped around the globe in a cone:

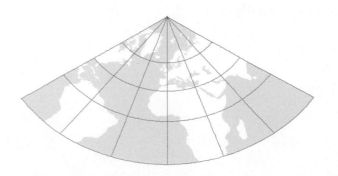

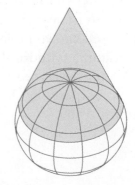

Most projections in use today begin as cylindrical, azimuthal, or conic shapes, and are mathematically modified to better preserve aspects of the graticule.

The Search for a Political View of the World

There are hundreds of map projections available for us to use, each suited for different purposes depending on their qualities. Geographers portraying the nations of the Western hemisphere often choose the Transverse Mercator Projection, for example. The nations of the African continent are often depicted by the Azimuthal Equal-Area Projection. For the whole earth, physical geographers sometimes favor Goode's World Projection because of its ability to depict the connectivity of landforms on the earth's surface.

When it comes to depicting global political geography, however, the process becomes tougher. The choice of projection for showing the nations of the world and their relationship to each other is one of the most heated cartographic debates to come to the public's attention.

The source of the debate stems from two projections. Perhaps the most well-known projection is the Mercator, a cylindrical projection originally developed for navigational purposes by Gerhard Mercator in 1569.

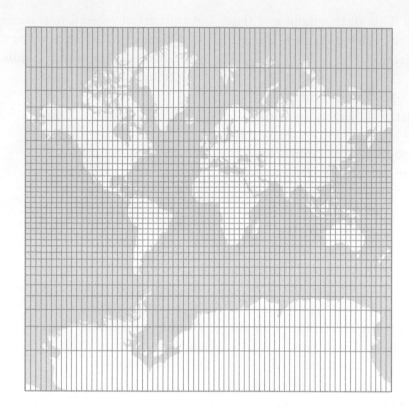

The **Mercator projection** preserves the graticule property of direction while forsaking area and shape. In part because it is easy to make, the Mercator has become a popularly reprinted wallmap for schools. Its utility for educational purposes, however, is dubious, because maintaining perfect direction creates significant distortion of shape and area. In the equatorial region, the distortion is minimal. In the high latitudes, however, the shape and size of landmasses are significantly distorted.

Another projection that became widespread during the twentieth century was the Van der Grinten, the official projection of the National Geographic Society. The Van der Grinten also depicted large amounts of distortion in the high latitudes.

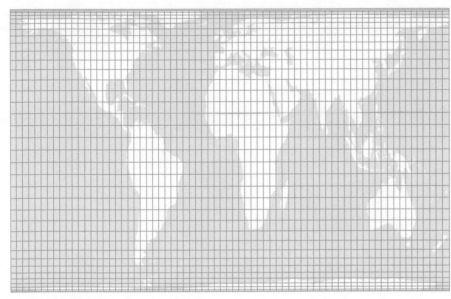

Gall-Peters Projection.

The dismal popular choices for looking at world political geography bothered Arno Peters, for whom the distortions comprised a social injustice of misrepresentation to the marginalized countries of the world. To Peters, political geography could be served only by preserving the property of area above all other properties of the graticule.

In 1972, dissatisfied with the conventional displays of distortions, he developed what he called the Peters Projection (now referred to as the Gall-Peters projection because of its derivation from a map by James Gall in 1855). The Peters map depicted the countries of the world in proportionate area in order to better represent developing countries in relationship to the developed world.

Question 1: Study the coastlines as they are depicted in the Mercator projection, and compare these to the Gall-Peters projection. Where are the maps most different?

Question 2: Is there any region or country that appears the same in both the Mercator and the Gall-Peters? Why is that?

Question 3: Do you agree that area is the most important criterion for comparing the spatial relationship between countries? What other characteristics besides physical size might be useful for making comparisons between political entities like countries and provinces?

Peters' map was embraced by relief organizations such as UNICEF and the World Health Organization, in which there was great interest in fair cartographic representation for developing nations. Today, it continues to be a popular wallmap.

Cartographers, on the other hand, have reacted negatively to Peters' map. For some, Peters' map is aesthetically offensive. Others have found it unacceptable as a world map because it preserves only one of the graticule's properties, an extreme solution for a map of the whole earth. This poor academic reception aside, Peters' map revitalized the cartographic debate over best fit solutions for projections of the political world. Because area, distance, direction, and shape are all important factors in the way a country is depicted, many cartographers now advocate that, for a general world political map, a compromise is necessary.

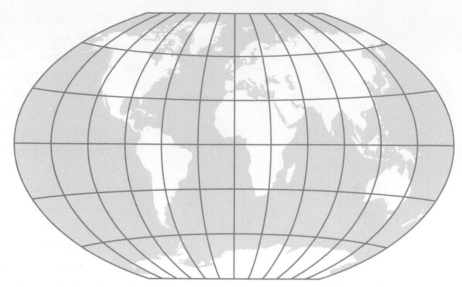

Winkel Tripel Projection.

Compromise, Compromise

After Peters, work on development of a better all-purpose world map projection was revitalized, and cartographers called for a rethinking of the benefits of the compromise projection.

A compromise projection preserves none of the properties of the graticule. Instead, it minimally distorts all properties in order to achieve a balance, or compromise, of distortions across the map. The current projection advocated by the National Geographic Society, the **Winkel Tripel,** is just such a compromise projection.

The Winkel Tripel is a modified azimuthal projection created by Oswald Winkel in 1921 as a middle ground between two other projections, the Equidis-tant Cylindrical and the Aitoff. In 1998, the National Geographic Society adopted it as the new standard for their world maps. The Winkel Tripel minimizes the distortion of shape, area, and direction, except in the very high latitudes at the poles. Just as Mercator's projection met the need for world maps in the sixteenth century to depict the earth in a way that would preserve the property of direction above all other graticule properties, the Winkel Tripel meets the current need for a world map to depict all of the earth except the polar regions by balancing shape, area, and direction distortions as evenly as possible.

Question 4: Compare the coastlines of the Winkel Tripel to a globe in your classroom. What compromises have been made in this map?

Question 5: What is the most important property of a country to preserve in a map?

Question 6: What will be the priorities of world projections twenty years from now as globalization intensifies?

Question 7: To what degree should aesthetics play a role in the creation of a political world map?

⊕ 6.2
Evaluating Redistricting Online

Another aspect of political geography in which mapping plays a primary role is **redistricting.** Redistricting is the process of creating new electoral district boundaries, which in turn creates new **electoral regions.**

As you have learned in class, new electoral district boundaries may be illegally manipulated or **gerrymandered** to favor certain sectors of society, such as political parties, ethnic groups, or age groups.

According to U.S. law, all states and counties with more than one electoral district must redistrict every ten years, to reflect new population figures released by the U.S. Census. Finding a way to redistrict so as to represent every citizen fairly, without gerrymandering, is a complex task of analyzing the geography of race, age, and political persuasion in a given district.

In this exercise we will analyze electoral redistricting in Hillsborough County, Florida, and compare the redistricting maps to the demographic characteristics of the county.

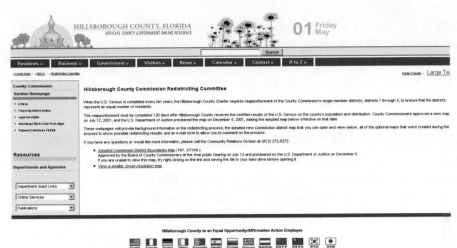

Screenshot courtesy of Hillsborough County Geographic Information Systems, 2009.

Step 1   Launch your browser and navigate to the *Hillsborough County Commission Redistricting* link under Exercise 6.2 in the "Exploring Human Geography with Maps" section of the *Human Mosaic* Web site.

This will take you to the home page shown above. This Web site describes the redistricting process that Hillsborough County underwent in 2001 for the reapportionment of its County Commission.

Step 2   In the text box on the left, click on the "Criteria" link under the "County Commission Section Homepage" to read about the criteria for redistricting the County Commission.

Question 1: Briefly summarize the main criteria that Hillsborough County considered in its redistricting process.

Step 3 In the same text box you used in Step 2, click on the "Proposed Commission Districts" link. As you scroll down this page, you will see where the Commission has posted the various maps or "plans" of new district boundaries submitted for consideration. They can be downloaded and opened as PDF files using Adobe Acrobat.

Three of these plans, with their corresponding population data tables, appear on the opposite page. In the maps, the old district boundaries are depicted as red and white lines, and the proposed new districts are depicted as shaded areas of different colors.

Question 2: Compare the old district boundaries in each of the three maps, B, D, and G. Which district is the most compact? What geographical factors (physical or human) might have influenced the shape of this district?

Question 3: Which of the former electoral districts is the least compact? What geographical factors might have influenced this shape?

Question 4: Compare the shapes of the proposed district boundaries in each of the three maps. Which of the three plans shows the greatest compactness?

Question 5: Evaluate the data on race in the tables to the right of the maps. Is there one plan that particularly favors the Hispanic vote? Why or why not?

Question 6: How would you evaluate the plans in terms of the African-American vote?

Next, let's see if we can learn more about the districts by comparing the proposed district plans to census data.

Step 4 Leave the Hillsborough County site and navigate to the "American FactFinder" link under Exercise 6.2 in the "Exploring Human Geography with Maps" section of the *Human Mosaic* Web site.

Step 5 From the FactFinder page, scroll down to the Maps link and click on "Thematic Maps (data)."

Step 6 Near the center of the page, click on the "Data Sets with Thematic Maps" link. This launches the interactive map application in FactFinder.

Step 7 In the "Select a Data Set" window choose "Census 2000 Summary File 1 (SF 1) 100-Percent Data" and click "Next." From the "Select Geography" window, choose "County" under "geographic type," then select Florida and Hillsborough County. Click the "Show Results" button after making your selections.

Step 8 Choose the "by subject" tab as the theme selection method and go to the "Population and Housing Unit Totals and GeographicConcepts" subject category, choose "Population

Density," and click "Search." The search will return a list of all available population density themes to portray in the map. Choose the "Persons per Square Mile: 2000" theme, and click the "Show Result" button.

You should now see a map of persons per square mile for Hillsborough County, Florida, in 2000, as in the screenshot below.

Screenshot from U.S. Census Bureau, American FactFinder (http://factfinder.census.gov), 2009.

You already have information about race for each of the districts. Are there other socioeconomic factors that might be considered in the districts? Below, we will explore two other demographic variables, age and income, to see if there is a correlation.

Step 9 Go to the horizontal "You are here:" menu bar and click on "Themes."

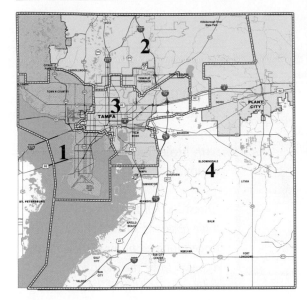

Plan B

	Total Population	White*	African-American	Native American	Asian-American	Other	Hispanic**	Non-Hispanic
DISTRICT 1	249,775	204,263 (82%)	17,893 (7%)	829 (0.3%)	7,906 (3%)	18,690 (7%)	56,383 (23%)	193,392 (77%)
DISTRICT 2	249,708	200,210 (80%)	25,115 (10%)	856 (0.3%)	6,901 (3%)	16,477 (7%)	36,278 (15%)	213,430 (85%)
DISTRICT 3	249,777	133,700 (54%)	91,107 (36%)	1,139 (0.5%)	3,453 (1%)	20,161 (8%)	52,950 (21%)	197,187 (79%)
DISTRICT 4	249,688	212,730 (85%)	15,308 (6%)	1,055 (0.4%)	3,687 (1%)	16,741 (7%)	34,081 (14%)	215,607 (86%)
Total	998,948							

* Numbers shown in parenthesis represent percentage of racial classification by district. Percentages may not equal 100% when added due to rounding.

** Americans of Hispanic or Latino decent are considered members of a language or ethnic minority.

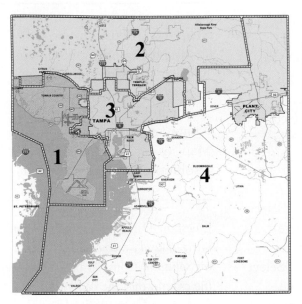

Plan D

	Total Population	White*	African-American	Native American	Asian-American	Other	Hispanic**	Non-Hispanic
DISTRICT 1	249,106	199,421 (80%)	21,041 (8%)	833 (0.3%)	7,686 (3%)	20,125 (8%)	64,407 (26%)	184,699 (74%)
DISTRICT 2	250,026	209,676 (84%)	18,821 (8%)	836 (0.3%)	6,976 (3%)	13,717 (5%)	31,478 (13%)	218,548 (87%)
DISTRICT 3	249,976	129,439 (52%)	94,923 (38%)	1,175 (0.5%)	3,640 (1%)	20,799 (8%)	47,000 (19%)	202,976 (81%)
DISTRICT 4	249,840	212,367 (85%)	14,638 (6%)	1,035 (0.4%)	3,645 (1%)	18,155 (7%)	36,807 (15%)	213,033 (85%)
Total	998,948							

* Numbers shown in parenthesis represent percentage of racial classification by district. Percentages may not equal 100% when added due to rounding.

** Americans of Hispanic or Latino decent are considered members of a language or ethnic minority.

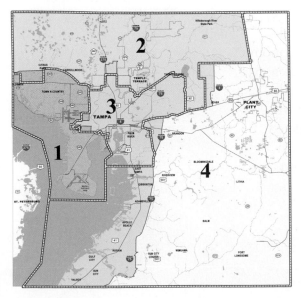

Plan G

	Total Population	White*	African-American	Native American	Asian-American	Other	Hispanic**	Non-Hispanic
DISTRICT 1	247,212	199,492 (81%)	19,239 (8%)	831 (0.3%)	7,685 (3%)	19,965 (8%)	62,764 (25%)	184,448 (75%)
DISTRICT 2	249,441	249,441 (83%)	20,126 (8%)	875 (0.4%)	8,013 (3%)	12,915 (5%)	32,399 (13%)	217,042 (87%)
DISTRICT 3	249,069	132,763 (53%)	91,583 (37%)	1,194 (0.5%)	2,580 (1%)	20,949 (8%)	48,614 (20%)	200,455 (80%)
DISTRICT 4	253,226	211,136 (83%)	18,475 (7%)	979 (0.4%)	3,669 (1%)	18,967 (7%)	35,915 (14%)	217,311 (86%)
Total	998,948							

* Numbers shown in parenthesis represent percentage of racial classification by district. Percentages may not equal 100% when added due to rounding.

** Americans of Hispanic or Latino decent are considered members of a language or ethnic minority.

Plans B, D, and G courtesy of Hillsborough County Geographic Information Systems.

Step 10 Choose "by subject" as the theme selection method. Go to the "Social Characteristics" subject category, choose "Older Population," and click "Search." The search will return a list of available themes related to older persons.

Step 11 From the list of themes choose "Percent of Persons 65 Years and Over: 2000" and click the "Show Result" button.

Question 7: What is the enumeration unit of this map?

Step 12 Because we want to look at the most detailed information that we can, change the enumeration unit to Block Group from the "Display map by:" pull-down menu located above the map.

In U.S. Census data, a **block group** is one of the smallest enumeration units available, averaging about 1,500 people in size.

You should now have a view of the redistricting area showing percent 65 and over by block group, as in the screenshot above.

Question 8: Compare the Census map with the proposed district boundary maps. (Remember that you can use the zoom and pan tools to explore different regions of the county.) Are there any districts that appear to favor people over the age of 65? If so, explain.

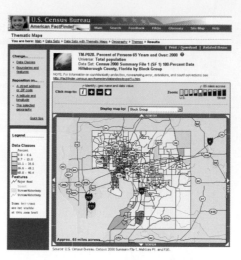

Screenshot from U.S. Census Bureau Web site, American FactFinder (http:/factfinder.census.gov), 2009.

Step 13 Return to the "You are here:" menu bar but this time click on the "Data Sets with Thematic Maps" link. Select "Census 2000 Summary File 3 (SF 3)—Sample Data" and click "Next."

Step 14 As before, for "Select a Geographic Type," choose "County"; for "Select a State," choose "Florida"; and for "Select a Geographic Area," choose "Hillsborough County" and click "Next."

Step 15 Choose "by subject," but this time go to the "Economic Characteristics" subject category, choose "Income (Individuals)," and click "Search" to return a list of all available income-related themes. Choose "Per Capita Income in 1999: 2000" and click "Show Result."

Question 9: Compare the map of per capita income to the proposed district boundary plans. Are there any districts that appear to favor people with higher incomes? Explain your reasoning.

Question 10: Based on what you have observed so far, which of the three proposed plans do you think appears to be the most equitable redistricting solution and why?

Step 16 Return to the Hillsborough County Commission Redistricting Committee Web page as in Step 1, and click on the link to the "Adopted Commission District Boundaries Map" (you can use the lower-resolution map link if you like).

Question 11: Do you think the committee found an equitable redistricting solution? Consider in your answer the criteria that the committee set forth, from Question 1, above.

⊛ ◉ 6.3
Political Boundaries, Generalization, and Scale

When we read a map for information about political boundaries and borders, we are dependent on the mapmaker's skill with **generalization.** Generalization is simply the term used by cartographers for the process of deciding how much geographical detail is going to be shown in a map. All maps are generalizations, because all maps are scaled-down versions of reality.

The level at which a political boundary is generalized on a map depends on the scale of the map (How much room is there to show these boundary details?), the quality of the original data (How much detail was known about the boundary to begin with?), and the intentions of the cartographer (Whose political claim is being shown?).

The balance that is struck between these factors can be a precarious one. The omission of a detail about one curve in an international border may result in inaccurate decision making, or cause grave offense for one or both countries.

The border between Eritrea and Ethiopia is a good example of how cartographic generalization can affect the relations between countries. Until 1952, Eritrea was a colony of Italy. Eritrea became independent from Italy following the Second World War, and in 1962, Ethiopia annexed the region as its new, northern province.

The map below is from a world atlas published in 1952, when Eritrea was on the eve of independence from Italy.

Question 1: Compare the difference in boundary-line symbolization between Ethiopia's northern border with Eritrea and its western border with Sudan. How has the cartographer differentiated these two kinds of boundaries?

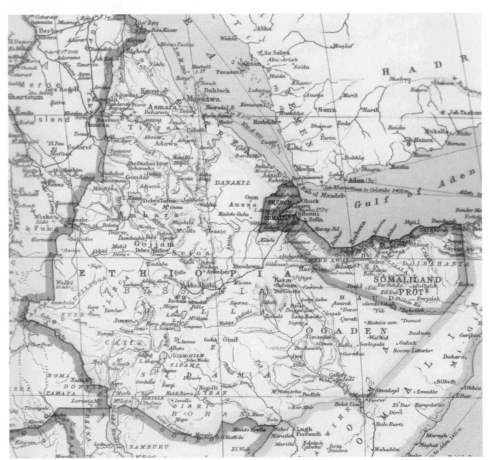

Detail from "Africa, North-East," in *The Citizen's Atlas of the World.* 10th ed. ©Bartholemew Ltd 1952. Reproduced by kind permission of HarperCollins Publishers, www.bartholemewmaps.com.

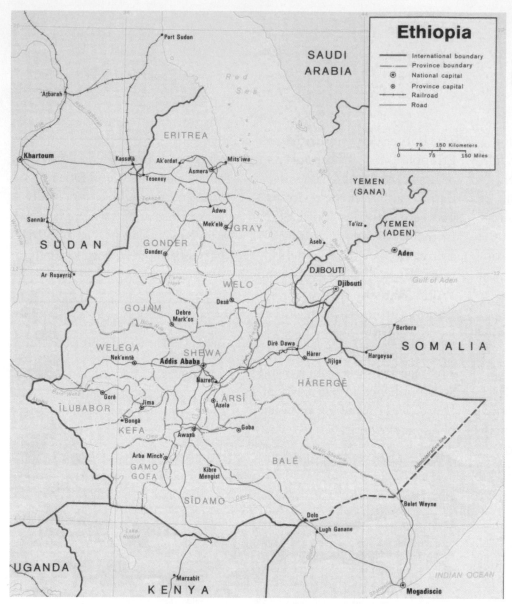

"Ethiopia." Base 504020, Central Intelligence Agency, Government Printing Office, January 1979.

In the map above, showing the same region in 1979, Ethiopia has been transformed by the 1962 annexation of Eritrea. The old international border is now a **relic boundary.**

Question 2: Compare the 1951 and 1979 maps of Ethiopia. How has the annexation changed Ethiopia's geographical context in the Horn of Africa? What advantages or disadvantages can you see for the people of Ethiopia? For the people of Eritrea?

Question 3: Can you find any indication in the 1979 map that there used to be an international border at what is now the provincial border of Eritrea, Tigray, and Gonder?

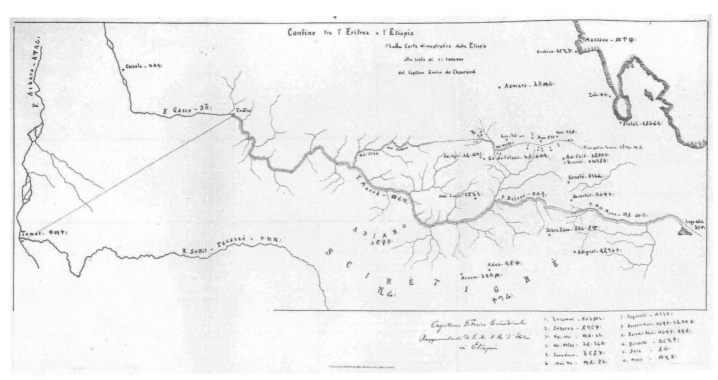

1900 Treaty Map, Eritrea-Ethiopia Boundary Commission, United Nations. EEBC Web site (www.un.org./Newlinks/eebcarbitration/), 2002.

Generalization and Interpretation

In 1993, Eritrea asserted its independence from Ethiopia. When this political independence extended to economic autonomy through the issuing of Eritrean currency in 1998, war broke out between the two countries.

The main dispute in the war centered on the delineation of the Eritrean-Ethiopian international border. The border was based on the old colonial boundaries of Eritrea as set by a 1900 Italian treaty, shown above. In the treaty, the border was described and graphically portrayed with a high degree of generalization, with the understanding that a more detailed map would be produced later.

Question 4: *Study the treaty map above. How is the colonial boundary depicted? Is this a natural, ethnographic, or geometric boundary?*

Despite its provisional nature, a less generalized map of the border was never produced, and the treaty map remained the primary description for the border. As a result, each country interpreted the specifics of the boundary location differently.

The conflicting interpretations are illustrated in these three maps from the Eritrea-Ethiopia Boundary Commission of the United Nations.

In the maps, the pink line represents Ethiopia's border claim, and the green line represents Eritrea's border claim.

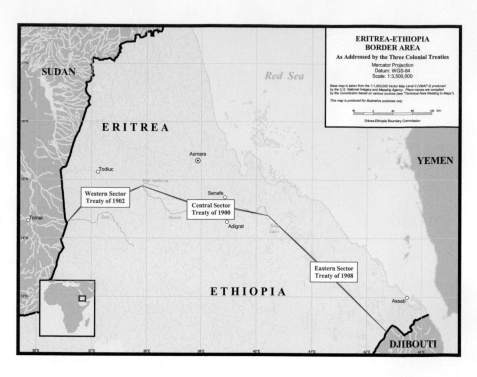

Question 5: Which segments of the border seem to be under the greatest dispute between the two countries: the Western Sector, the Central Sector, or the Eastern Sector?

Question 6: Look back to the treaty map on the previous page and see if you can relate the sectors to the colonial illustration. Which aspects of the treaty map seem to be causing the greatest conflict?

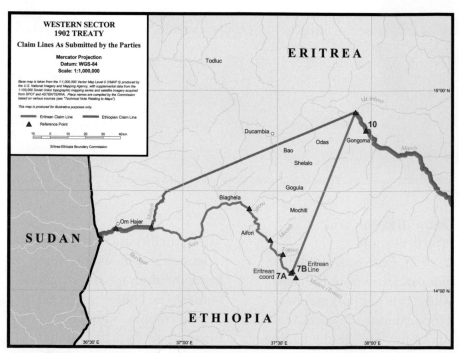

"Eritrea-Ethiopia Border Area," top, and "Western Sector 1902 Treaty," bottom, from Eritrea-Ethiopia Boundary Commission, United Nations. EEBC Web site (www.un.org./NewLinks/eebcarbitration/), 2002.

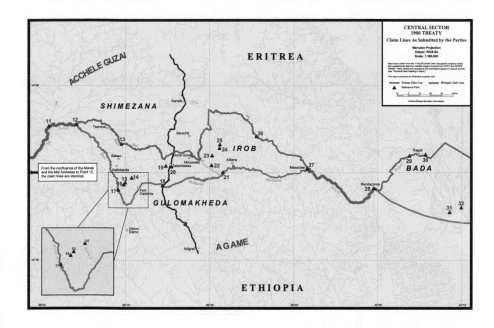

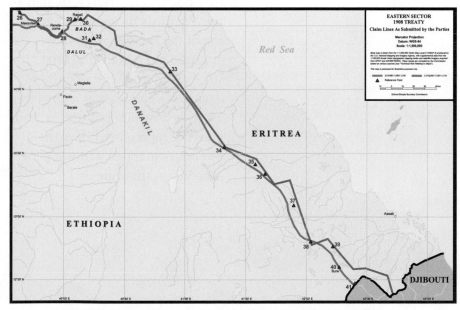

"Central Sector 1902 Treaty," top, and "Eastern Sector 1902 Treaty," bottom, from Eritrea-Ethiopia Boundary Commission, United Nations. EEBC Web site (www.un.org./ NewLinks/eebcarbitration/), 2002.

After 80,000 lives were lost in this conflict, a peace agreement between the two countries was finally forged in December 2000, and a commission was established to make an objective ruling on the border. The Eritrea-Ethiopia Boundary Commission studied the treaty map and border description carefully, and in April 2002, released a more specific description of the border, divided according to the three sectors of the previous maps. As of 2009, both countries have not agreed on how to implement the boundary commission's decision.

In Search of a New Border

For the last part of this exercise, imagine that you are in the boundary drawing seat of the commission, implementing the new boundary as mandated by the United Nations.

Step 1   Photocopy the three blank base maps, one for each of the three sectors, on the next five pages.

Step 2   For each sector, read the new description of the boundary as handed down by the commission on pp. 87–88 and plot the new delineation of the Eritrea-Ethiopia border on the corresponding base map of the region.

Question 7: Analyze the three new sector maps you have created, and compare them to the old boundary map. Is this new international boundary more geometric? More natural?

Question 8: Will there be a new relic political boundary? If so, where?

Question 9: Compare the new boundary to the previous claims of Eritrea and Ethiopia. Where did Eritrea make concessions to Ethiopia? Did Ethiopia in turn make concessions to Etritrea?

You will notice that there are several turning points from the border description that remain vague. The final stage of setting a new political boundary, demarcation, consists in the actual marking of the boundary on the ground, and it is in this final stage when these last details are decided. Demarcation is the largest scale at which political boundaries are represented. It is the boundary mapped without generalization at the scale of 1:1.

Decision

For the reasons set out above, the Commission unanimously decides that the line of the boundary between Eritrea and Ethiopia is as follows:

A. In the Western Sector

(i) The boundary begins at the tripoint between Eritrea, Ethiopia and the Sudan and then runs into the centre of the Setit opposite that point (Point 1).

(ii) The boundary then follows the Setit eastwards to its confluence with the Tomsa (Point 6).

(iii) At that point, the boundary turns to the northeast and runs in a straight line to the confluence of the Mareb and the Mai Ambessa (Point 9).

B. In the Central Sector

(i) The boundary begins at the confluence of the Mareb and the Mai Ambessa (Point 9).

(ii) It follows the Mareb eastwards to its confluence with the Belesa (Point 11).

(iii) Thence it runs upstream the Belesa to the point where the Belesa is joined by the Belesa A and the Belesa B (Point 12).

(iv) To the east and southeast of Point 12, the boundary ascends the Belesa B, diverging from that river so as to leave Tserona and its environs to Eritrea. The boundary runs round Tserona at a distance of approximately one kilometre from its current outer edge, in a manner to be determined more precisely during demarcation.

(v) Thereafter, upon rejoining the Belesa B, the boundary continues southward up that river to Point 14, where it turns to the southwest to pass up the unnamed tributary flowing from that direction, to the source of that tributary at Point 15. From that point it crosses the watershed by a straight line to the source of a tributary of the Belesa A at Point 16 and passes down that tributary to its confluence with the Belesa A at Point 17. It then continues up the Belesa A to follow the Eritrean claim line to Point 18 so as to leave Ford Cadorna and its environs within Eritrea.... Point 18 lies 100 metres west of the centre of the road running from Adigrat to Zalambessa.

(vi) From Point 18, the boundary runs parallel to the road at a distance of 100 metres from its centre along its western side and in the direction of Zalambessa until about one kilometre south of the current outer edge of the town. In order to leave that town and its environs to Ethiopia, the boundary turns to the northwest to pass around Zalambessa at a distance of approximately one kilometre from its current outer edge until the boundary rejoins the Treaty line at approximately Point 20, but leaving the location of the former Eritrean customs post within Eritrea. The current outer edge of Zalambessa will be determined more precisely during the demarcation.

(vii) From Point 20 the boundary passes down the Muna until it meets the Enda Dashim at Point 21.

(viii) At Point 21 the boundary turns to the northwest to follow the Enda Dashim upstream to Point 22. There the boundary leaves that river to pass northwards along one of its tributaries to Point 23. There the boundary turns northeastwards to follow a higher tributary to its source at Point 24.

(ix) At Point 24 the boundary passes in a straight line overland to Point 25, the source of one of the headwaters of a tributary of the Endeli, whence it continues along that tributary to Point 26, where it joins the Endeli.

(x) From Point 26, the boundary descends the Endeli to its confluence with the Muna at Point 27.

(xi) From Point 27, the boundary follows the Muna/Endeli downstream. Near Rendacoma, at approximately Point 28, the river begins also to be called the Ragali.

(xii) From Point 28, the line continues down the Muna/Endeli/Ragali to Point 29, northwest of the Salt Lake, and thence by straight lines to Points 30 and 31, at which last point this sector of the boundary terminates.

C. In the Eastern Sector

The boundary begins at Point 31 and then continues by a series of straight lines connecting ten points, Points 32 and 41. Point 41 will be at the boundary with Djibouti. Point 40, lies equidistantly between the two checkpoints at Bure.

— Eritrea-Ethiopia Boundary Commission,
Decision Regarding Delimitation of the Border between The State of Eritrea and The Federal Democratic Republic of Ethiopia, April 13, 2002.

Maps on pp. 89–91 (Western Sector," "Central Sector," and "Eastern Sector") adapted from Eritrea-Ethiopia Boundary Commission, United Nations. EEBC Web site (www.un.org./NewLinks/eebcarbitration/), 2002.

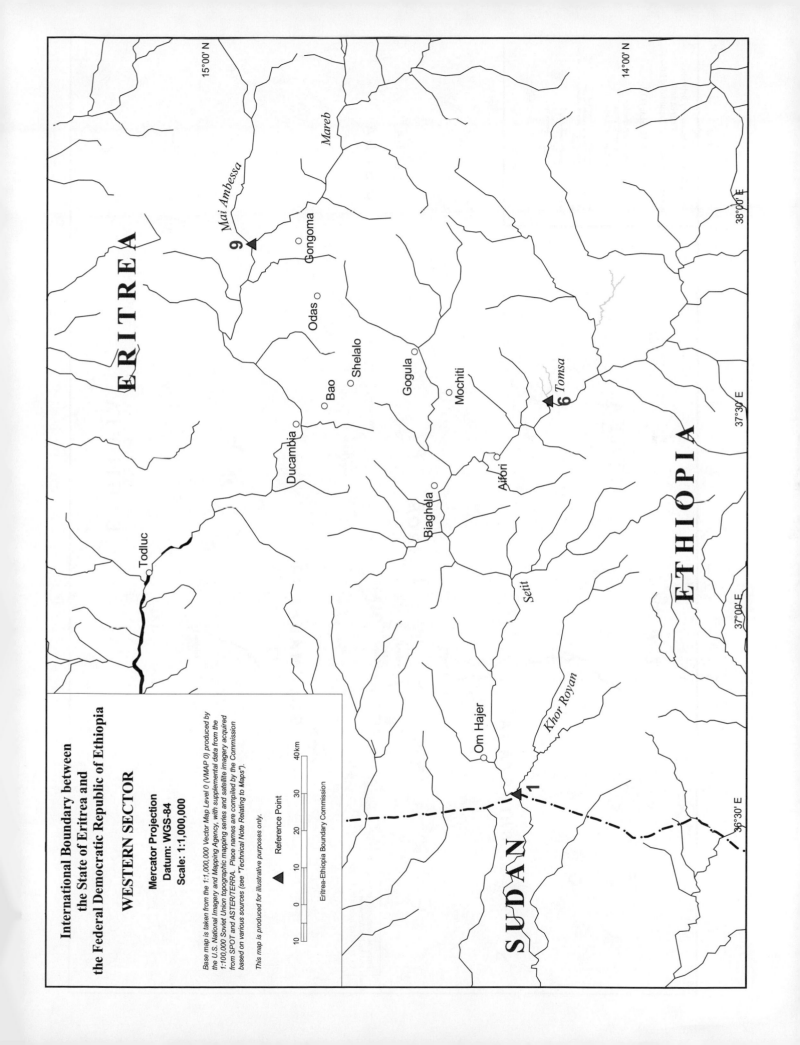

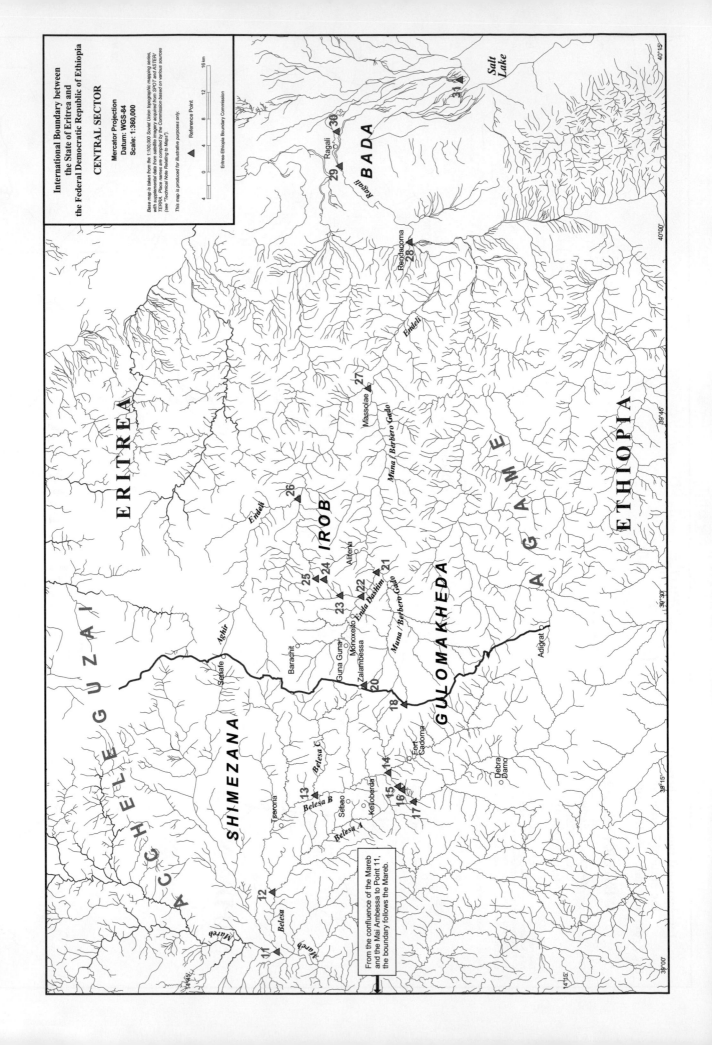

International Boundary between
the State of Eritrea and
the Federal Democratic Republic of Ethiopia

CENTRAL SECTOR

Mercator Projection
Datum: WGS-84
Scale: 1:360,000

Base map is taken from the 1:100,000 Soviet Union topographic mapping series,
with supplemental data from satellite imagery acquired from SPOT and ASTER/
TERRA. Place names are compiled by the Commission based on various sources
(see "Technical Note Relating to Maps").

This map is produced for illustrative purposes only.

▲ Reference Point

Eritrea-Ethiopia Boundary Commission

From the confluence of the Mareb
and the Mai Ambessa to Point 11,
the boundary follows the Mareb.

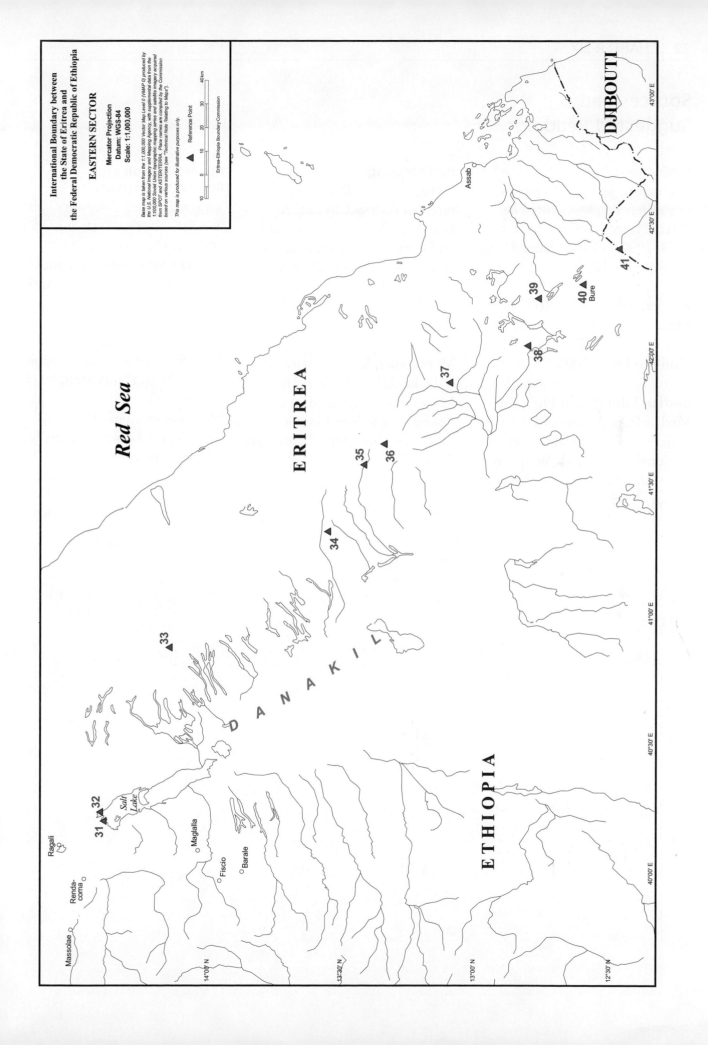

International Boundary between
the State of Eritrea and
the Federal Democratic Republic of Ethiopia

EASTERN SECTOR

Mercator Projection
Datum: WGS-84
Scale: 1:1,000,000

Base map is taken from the 1:1,000,000 Vector Map Level 0 (VMAP 0) produced by
the U.S. National Imagery and Mapping Agency, with supplemental data from the
1:100,000 Soviet Union topographic mapping series and satellite imagery acquired
from SPOT and ASTER/TERRA. Place names are compiled by the Commission
based on various sources (see "Technical Note 'Relating to Maps'").

This map is produced for illustrative purposes only.

▲ Reference Point

Eritrea-Ethiopia Boundary Commission

Red Sea

ERITREA

DANAKIL

ETHIOPIA

DJIBOUTI

Assab

Bure

Massolae

Renda-
coma

Ragali

Salt
Lake

Maglalla

Fiscio

Barale

14°00' N

13°30' N

13°00' N

12°30' N

40°00' E

40°30' E

41°00' E

41°30' E

42°00' E

42°30' E

43°00' E

31
32
33
34
35
36
37
38
39
40
41

Sources and Suggested Readings

Projections

Crampton, Jeremy. "Cartography's Defining Moment: The Peters Projection Controversy 1974–1990." *Cartographica* 31 No. 4 (1994):16–32.

Krygier, John and Denis Wood. *Making Maps: A Visual Guide to Map Design for GIS*. New York: Guilford Press, 2005.

Snyder, John P., and Philip M. Voxland. *An Album of Map Projections*. U.S. Geological Survey Professional Paper 1453. Washington, D.C.: Government Printing Office, 1989.

Redistricting

Horn, Mark. "GIS and the Geography of Politics," in Paul A. Longley, Michael F. Goodchild, and David J. Maguire, et al., eds. *Geographical Information Systems*. Volume 2: Management Issues and Applications. 2nd ed. N.Y.: Wiley, 1999.

Monmonier, Mark. *Bushmanders & Bullwinkles: How Politicians Manipulate Electronic Maps and Census Data to Win Elections*. Chicago: The University of Chicago Press, 2001.

Generalization and Boundary Disputes

Eritrea-Ethiopia Boundary Commission. *Decision Regarding Delimitation of the Border between the State of Eritrea and the Federal Democratic Republic of Ethiopia*. April 2002.

Monmonier, Mark. *Drawing the Line: Tales of Maps and Cartocontroversy*. N.Y.: Henry Holt, 1995.

Monmonier, Mark. *How to Lie with Maps*. Chicago: University of Chicago Press, 1991.

CHAPTER

7

Religion

Vocabulary applied in this chapter
Islam
religious culture region
adherents
diffusion
sacred space
pilgrimage

New vocabulary
general map
thematic map
dot distribution map
proportional symbol map
aggregated data
count vs. proportional data
spiritual map

⊕ 7.1
A Closer Look at the Thematic Map

Geographers tend to think of maps as belonging to one of two categories: **general** or **thematic.** A **general map** depicts the locations of a range of geographical features without emphasizing any particular feature. General maps are crucial sources for exploring the cultural geography of a place (the Ordnance Survey maps you studied in Chapter 2 are good examples of general maps).

A **thematic map,** on the other hand, emphasizes a theme by showing the distribution of one or two particular features in a region. The thematic map is a fundamental tool for presenting ideas and findings about specific

Country	% Muslim	Country	% Muslim	Country	% Muslim	Country	% Muslim
Afghanistan	99	East Timor	1	Lebanon	55	Senegal	94
Albania	70	Ecuador	0	Lesotho	1	Serbia	3.2
Algeria	99	Egypt	90	Liberia	20	Seychelles	0.2
Angola	0.7	El Salvador	0	Libya	97	Sierra Leone	60
Argentina	1.5	Eritrea	48	Lithuania	0.1	Singapore	15
Armenia	no data	Estonia	0.4	Luxembourg	2	Slovakia	0.1
Australia	1.7	Ethiopia	32.8	Republic of Macedonia	32	Slovenia	2.4
Austria	4.2	Fiji	7	Madagascar	7	Solomon Islands	0
Azerbaijan	93.4	Finland	0.4	Malawi	20	Somalia	99.9
Bahrain	98	France	10	Malaysia	60.4	South Africa	1.5
Bangladesh	88.3	Gabon	1	Maldives	99.4	Spain	2.3
Belarus	0.1	Gambia	90	Mali	90	Sri Lanka	7
Belgium	4	Georgia	9.9	Mauritania	99.9	Sudan	70
Belize	0.6	Germany	3.9	Mauritius	17	Suriname	13.5
Benin	24.4	Ghana	15.6	Mexico	0.3	Swaziland	1
Bhutan	0.5	Greece	1.3	Moldova	0.1	Sweden	3
Bolivia	0	Grenada	0.3	Mongolia	4	Switzerland	4.3
Bosnia and Herzegovina	40	Guatemala	0	Montenegro	18	Syria	90
Botswana	0.2	Guinea	85	Morocco	98.7	Taiwan	0.3
Brazil	0	Guinea-Bissau	45	Mozambique	20	Tajikistan	90
Brunei	64	Guyana	7.2	Myanmar	4	Tanzania	40
Bulgaria	12.2	Haiti	0	Namibia	1	Thailand	4.6
Burkina Faso	50	Honduras	0	Nepal	4	Togo	13.7
Burundi	10	Hungary	0	Netherlands	6	Trinidad and Tobago	5.8
Cambodia	3.5	Iceland	0.1	New Caledonia	4	Tunisia	98
Cameroon	20	India	13.4	New Zealand	0.6	Turkey	99
Canada	2	Indonesia	88.2	Nicaragua	0	Turkmenistan	89
Central African Republic	15	Iran	98	Niger	80	Uganda	12.1
Chad	51	Iraq	97	Nigeria	50	Ukraine	1.1
Chile	0	Ireland	0.5	Norway	1.8	United Arab Emirates	76
China	1.5	Israel	12	Oman	92.7	United Kingdom	2.7
Colombia	0	Italy	1.4	Pakistan	97	United States	0.6
Comoros	98	Jamaica	0.2	Panama	0.3	Puerto Rico	0.1
Republic of the Congo	2	Japan	0.1	Papua New Guinea	0	Uruguay	0
Democratic Republic of the Congo	10	Jordan	95	Paraguay	0	Uzbekistan	88
Costa Rica	0.1	Kazakhstan	47	Peru	0	Vanuatu	0.1
Côte d'Ivoire	35	Kenya	10	Philippines	5	Venezuela	0.4
Croatia	1.3	Korea	no data	Poland	0	Vietnam	0.1
Cuba	0	South Korea	0.1	Portugal	0.3	West Bank and Gaza	83.7
Cyprus	18	Kosovo	90	Qatar	77.5	Western Sahara	99.8
Czech Republic	0.1	Kuwait	67.5	Romania	0.2	Yemen	99
Denmark	2	Kyrgyzstan	75	Russia	14	Zambia	0
Djibouti	94	Laos	0	Rwanda	4.6	Zimbabwe	0
Dominican Republic	0	Latvia	0	Saudi Arabia	100		

Central Intelligence Agency, *The World Factbook* July 2008, https://www.cia.gov/library/publications/the-world-factbook/index.html, accessed January 24, 2009; U.S. State Department *Background Notes*, http://www.state.gov/r/pa/ei/bgn/, accessed January 24, 2009.

topics in cultural geography to an audience. At this point, you have already worked with two types of thematic map, the choropleth and the isarithmic. In this exercise, we will take a closer look at how each type of thematic map works and how the type we choose affects the way in which we perceive the geographical distribution of culture.

Suppose that the theme you want to map is the global geography of **Islam**. The data table on the opposite page shows a percentage of population estimated to be Muslim, whether Sunni, Shi'a, or another Islamic denomination, for each country. In some cases, "0" indicates countries with estimated populations of less than one percent.

Question 1: Study the data in the table. Can you determine from this format which region of the world has the lowest percentage of Muslim population? Why or why not?

Before thematic maps were invented, mapmakers began with a base map of the world, and wrote the number of features inside each of the countries. In our case, the map would look like the one below.

As you can see, the more data you have, the less useful is the technique of placing numbers on maps. We can compare the countries by reading the numbers associated with them, but it is dif-

ficult to get an overall sense of the distribution of the data set. To get to the visual pattern of the information, geographers eventually replaced the written number with a graphic symbol, creating the tradition of the thematic map.

Despite the seemingly wide diversity of mapping in society, our choices for the thematic map type are somewhat limited. As Arthur Robinson has written, Western mapmakers have discovered only a limited number of ways to show thematic data on maps (all, incidentally, discovered by the end of the nineteenth century).

This exercise compares three of these thematic map types: the choropleth, the **dot distribution,** and the **proportional symbol.** (Another type of thematic map, the cartogram, is explored in Chapter 12, and in Chapter 3 you explored the strengths of the isarithmic map.)

The choropleth, the dot distribution, and the proportional symbol are similar in that they are all useful for displaying data that has been aggregated by enumeration unit. **Aggregated data** means that the data was collected from several locations within a region and then totaled or "aggregated" as a single data value for that region.

For example, in this exercise, the enumeration unit is a political unit: the countries of the world. Each country has a number associated with it, which represents the total percentage of the Muslim population from all villages, towns, and cities within that country.

As you learned in Chapter 3, a choropleth map shows geographical information over an area, using a pattern or color for each enumeration unit. The top map on the opposite page, which shows the percent of each country's population that is Muslim, is mapped by choropleth.

Question 2: How does the choropleth improve on the map using only numbers to show the distribution of Muslims?

Question 3: What information is lost?

The choropleth is one of the most popular techniques because it is simple to make with or without a computer. It is, thus, the type of thematic map you are most likely to see in human geography. Ease of construction does not always signify the best solution for mapping a particular geography, however.

For example, a correct choropleth shows **proportional data,** such as percent of population—or per capita—or per square mile. What if you wanted your map to show the total number of Muslim people in each country? Number of people is **count,** rather than proportional, data. For that type of data, the choropleth is not necessarily a good choice. In the bottom map on the opposite page, the choropleth is redrawn to depict the same data as count data.

Question 4: How do the two choropleth maps compare?

Question 5: How does the size of the country influence the data set in the second choropleth?

Question 6: How does the population of the country influence the data set in the second choropleth?

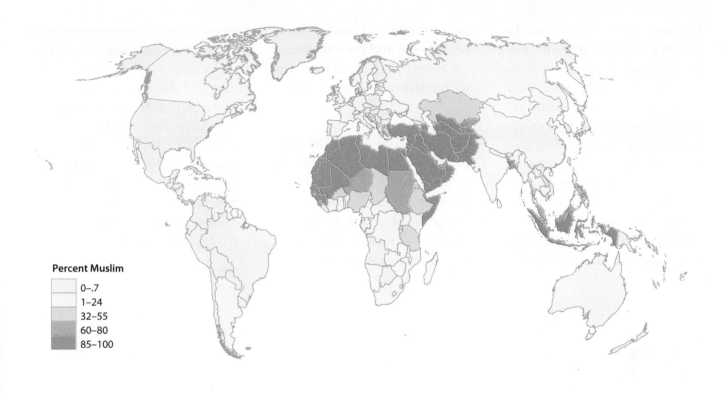

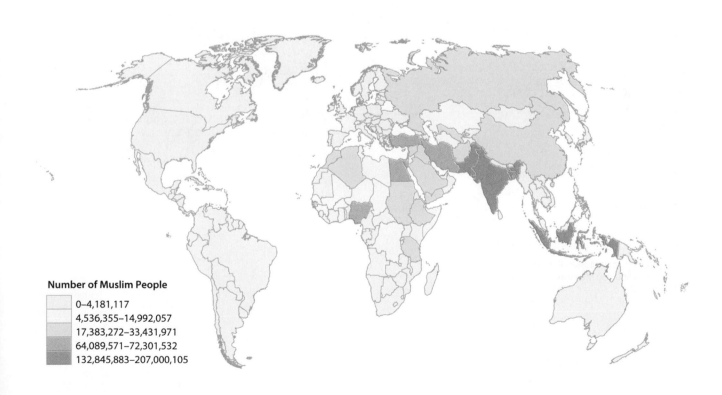

Another way to show count data is with a **dot distribution** or **dot density** map. As its name indicates, the dot distribution map uses dots to show the distribution of phenomena over an area. The placement of the dots does not show the actual location of the data, however. Dot distribution maps use dots placed randomly across an area to show the relative density of a feature. In the map below, each country is assigned a corresponding number of dots, and then the dots are placed in random locations within that particular country.

A third thematic technique for showing count data is the **proportional symbol map.** This type of map shows the number of phenomena in a particular area using a symbol scaled to represent that data, as in the bottom map on the opposite page.

Question 7: Compare the dot distribution map, the proportional symbol map, and the first choropleth. How do the maps differ in the spatial distribution pattern depicted in each?

Question 8: Which map do you think is the most useful for a detailed understanding of the geography of Muslim people? On what criteria do you base your opinion?

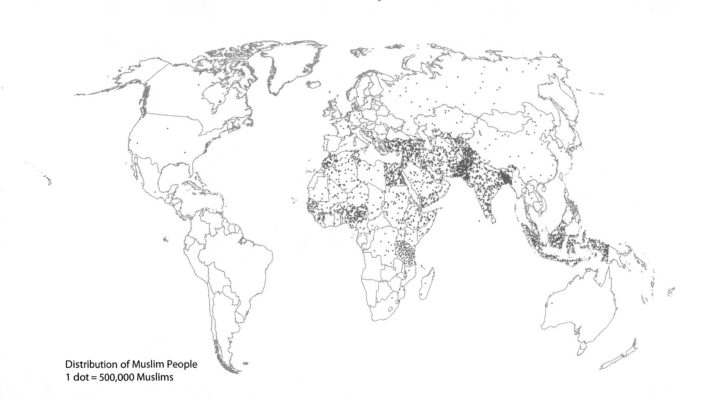

Distribution of Muslim People
1 dot = 500,000 Muslims

Question 9: Which would be the best choice for showing information quickly to an audience in a slide show? Why?

As you can see from the exercise, choosing a good areal thematic map is an art, a matter of informed judgment and considerable practice. Experimentation is important as is attention to the audience and medium for your final map. On some occasions it may be critical to include more than one kind of thematic map in order to properly represent the data.

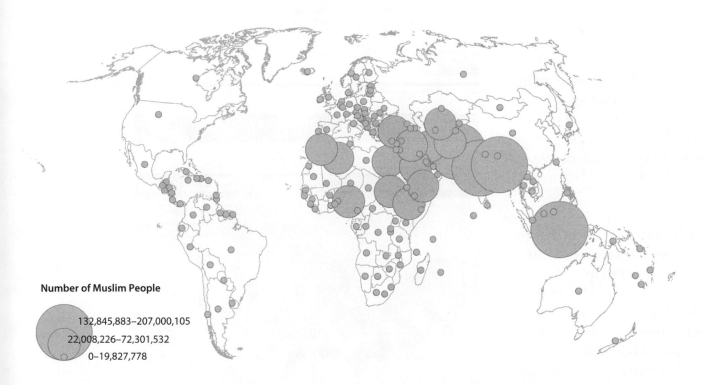

Number of Muslim People

132,845,883–207,000,105

22,008,226–72,301,532

0–19,827,778

⊕ 7.2
Adherents, Membership, and Sects

A map of the geography of religion may be based on any number of indicators of that religion. A map of **adherents** shows the proportion of the population that adheres to the religion whether or not they have formal ties to a religious institution. A map of membership, on the other hand, depicts those adherents that do have a formal affiliation with a religious institution.

The spatiality of religion can also be understood through mapping locations of objects in the visible landscape: the number and distribution of churches, for example, or the locations of shrines and other holy sites. Geographers try to find the combination of indicators that will best help to uncover spatiality.

Religion is particularly challenging, however, as Edwin Scott Gaustad and Philip L. Barlow note in their *New Historical Atlas of Religion in America*. Gaustad and Barlow note that there is no standard definition of church or other place of worship, nor of adherent, nor member. What makes a church? Is a child an adherent? The more information the map reader has about a particular faith and its records, the more likely an interpretation of the map can be made.

Screenshots © 2009 American Religious Data Archive Web site. Used with permission.

This exercise explores the geography of religion using an interactive map at the Association of Religious Data Archives (ARDA). Although the ARDA shows only the geography of Christianity in the United States, the site allows you to explore the spatiality of some 130 Christian sects.

Step 1 Launch your browser and navigate to the "Association of Religious Data Archives" link under Exercise 7.2 in the "Exploring Human Geography with Maps" section of the *Human Mosaic* Web site.

This will take you to the ARDA gateway page, as shown in the screenshot, top left.

Step 2 In the horizontal navigation bar near the top of the page, click on "GIS Maps." You should see a page similar to the middle screenshot on the left.

Step 3 Under "Select your map," select the "Religious Adherence Map" radio button, and click "Display Map." This will take you to a map of the United States that should look similar to the bottom screenshot.

From the pull-down menu labeled "Select map," browse the menus and sub-menus to examine religious groups and denominations. The atlas presents data for the years 1980, 1990, and 2000. You can explore the maps using the zoom feature in the tool bar and create a slideshow of the maps you view.

Step 4 For 2000, choose a major religious group or denomination from the pull-down menus. Choose a religion that has a strong regional basis in the United States. For example, you

have learned that the Mormons ("Church of Jesus Christ of Latter-day Saints" under the pull-down menu "Other Denominations") predominate in the intermountain West.

Step 5 For the major religious group or denomination of your choice, examine the map of its spatial distribution.

Question 1: Does the map depict a strong religious culture region for the religious group or denomination you chose?

Question 2: Does the region in the map conform to generalizations about that religion's culture region? How is it the same or different?

Exploring Evidence of Religious Diffusion
Religious cultural regions based on number of churches is a simple geographical concept to visualize, because it is static information with countable geographical features (number of churches). Religious **diffusion**, by contrast, is more difficult to display in a map because it involves movement, or the interpretation of movement.

The ARDA allow users to compile animated slide shows of its religious statistics. This allows us to get a sense of religious diffusion.

Step 6 For this exercise we will see if we can detect diffusion in the geography of Southern Baptists. Select "Religion, 1980" and "Evangelical Denominations" and "Southern Baptist Convention."

Question 3: Describe the regional differences for Southern Baptists that you observe on the map. Which region stands out as having the highest percentage of adherents? The lowest?

Question 4: Does the geography of Southern Baptists conform to the broad regional subdivisions of Northeast, Southeast, Midwest, Plains, Southwest, and Northwest? Why or why not?

Step 7 Beneath the legend for the Southern Baptists map, click the "create a slideshow" button. This opens a slideshow template that allows you to view multiple maps in succession. Click the first slide panel on the left to save the map of Southern Baptists in 1980.

Step 8 Change the year to 1990 and click the second slide panel to add the Southern Baptists 1990 map to your slideshow. Do the same for 2000.

Step 9 In the slideshow dialogue box (beneath the map legend), click on the stick figure of the human to turn on the animation feature. Doing so allows slides to seamlessly transition into the next rather than abruptly changing from slide to slide.

Step 10 Press the slideshow's play button and examine the changing spatial distribution of Southern Baptists between 1980 and 2000. You can adjust the speed of the show and allow it to loop rather than stopping after 2000.

Question 5: Describe the pattern that you see for each year. Where are the number of Southern Baptists growing and shrinking?

Question 6: Based on your description of the spatial distribution of Southern Baptists between 1980 and 2000, in what general ways is the Southern Baptist religion diffusing in the United States?

🌐 7.3
Maps for Pilgrims

Maps are useful for showing the material landscape of the sacred: the locations of shrines and the paths of religious pilgrimage.

But maps can also depict the experience of the sacred. Christians, Hindus, Jains, Buddhists, and Indigenous peoples around the world all use maps to depict the spaces of spiritual experience.

Spiritual maps are markedly different from both reference and thematic maps. Because the realm of the sacred is often perceived to be incompatible with the realm of the profane, maps of **sacred space** are sometimes composed according to different rules and aesthetic principles than conventional cartographic depictions of the same region. Sacred space, being fundamentally different from profane space, requires a separate cartographic language in order to express its separateness from profane space.

One example of the difference between the religious cartography of pilgrimage and nonreligious cartography comes from the city of Varanasi on the Ganges River in Uttar Pradesh, India.

Varanasi is the ancient "City of Light," the destination for Hindu pilgrims seeking renewal by washing away sins in the sacred Ganges River. Varanasi is also the place where Hindus can be released from samsara, the cycle of life and reincarnation, by dying in the holy space of the city, inside the gates. Known also as the city of Kashi, the name "Varanasi" derives from the names of the tributaries flowing into the Ganges at this place, the Varana and Asi rivers.

In 1876, Kailasanatha Sukula created a map of Varanasi intended to make the city, in his words, "constantly visible for foreigners." Today, a reproduction of Sukula's "Mirror of KÁĐÍ" is on the Web at the Varanasi Research Project— Visualized Space site.

Step 1 Launch your browser and navigate to the "Varanasi Research Project" at the link under Exercise 7.3 in the "Exploring Human Geography with Maps" section of the *Human Mosaic* Web site.

You should see the gateway to the Varanasi Research Project Web site as shown below.

Screenshots above and right © 2009 Dr. Jörg Gengnagel, Varanasi Research Project — Visualized Space. Used with permission of the author. Reproduction of the *Mirror of Kashi* by Kailasanatha Sukula used with permission of the British Library.

Step 2   From the yellow bar along the bottom of the Web site, click "The Map." This will take you to a clickable version of the Mirror of KÁÐÍ, as shown in the screenshot below.

At this site, the overall view of the map is shown in the small image in the lower right area of the page.

Step 3   Roll your cursor over the small overview map. The cursor will highlight gray sections of the map, each with its own index number. Each of these squares is an area that can be

zoomed in for better detail and displayed in the larger map area in the left side of the Web page.

Step 4   Take a moment to explore Sukula's map by clicking the individual squares and looking at the views that result.

In this map of Varanasi, the Ganges River is represented by a wide, textured river flowing across the lower half of the manuscript. Two narrower rivers are depicted flowing into the Ganges; these are the tributaries Varuna (squares 54 and 62) and Asi (square 42).

The large thin square at the center of the map symbolizes the gates of the city. Inside this square are the Viveswara temple, the main temple in the city, drawn with flags waving (squares 27–28 and 35–36), and the holy site of the Gyan Bapi well (square 36). Surrounding these central features, the city's religious sanctuaries radiate in a circular pattern.

Historian Jan Pieper studied Sukula's map and compared it to a British map created 50 years earlier by the surveyor and artist James Prinsep.

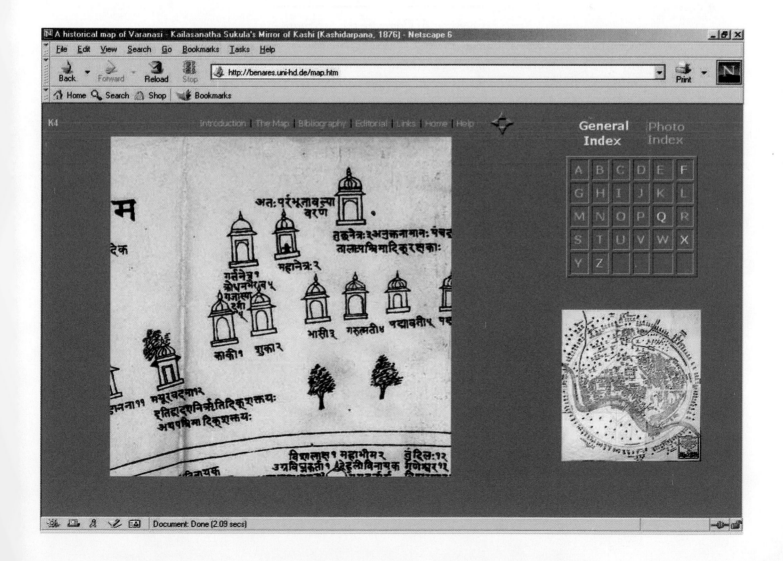

On the opposite page, a copy of Prinsep's map is reproduced. Prinsep also included the Ganges River, depicted as the eastern border of the city map, with the Varana and Asi rivers flowing into it. The Viveswara temple and Gyan Bapi well are also shown on the western banks of the Ganges.

In Pieper's study of the two maps, he points out that although both Sukula and Prinsep intend their maps to be read by visitors to Varanasi, each mapmaker depicts very different spaces of the city, one sacred and one profane, by using very different map symbols or codes.

For example, compare the difference in the way that architecture is depicted in the two maps.

Question 1: Study the symbols used by Sukula. How are buildings depicted? Based on these symbols, which do you think are the most important religious structures in this city? Which do you think are of lesser significance? Why?

Question 2: Compare the way that Prinsep symbolizes buildings. What differences do you observe?

Question 3: How are roads depicted differently in Sukula's map compared with Prinsep's map?

Question 4: How is perspective used in these two maps?

Question 5: What is the difference in the orientation of the two maps? In which direction is Prinsep's map oriented? In which direction is Sukula's map oriented?

The questions above explore the differences between sacred cartography and profane cartography by looking at the contrast in the way features are symbolized. But we can also study the differences by considering which features are included and which features are absent or not included in the two types of mapping.

Question 6: Compare the two maps again. What features of the geography of the city are shown in Prinsep's map that do not appear in Sukula's map? Why do you think this is?

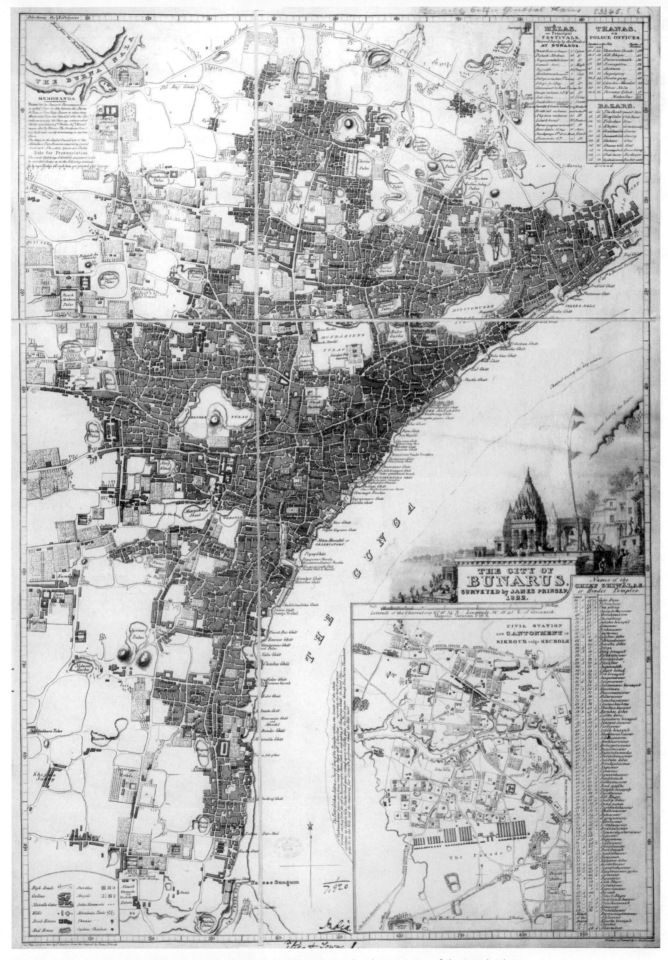

"The City of Bunarus" by James Prinsep. British Library Maps 53345(6). Used with permission of the British Library.

Sources and Suggested Readings

The Thematic Map

Robinson, Arthur. *Early Thematic Mapping in the History of Cartography.* Chicago: University of Chicago Press, 1982.

Petchenik, B. B. 1979. "From Place to Space: The Psychological Achievement of Thematic Mapping." *American Cartographer* 6: 5–12.

Krygier, John and Denis Wood, *Making Maps: A Visual Guide to Map Design for GIS.* New York: Guilford Press, 2005.

Adherents, Members, Sects

Gaustad, Edwin Scott, and Philip L. Barlow. *New Historical Atlas of Religion in America.* N.Y.: Oxford University Press, 2001.

Halvorson, Peter L. and William M. Newman. *Atlas of Religious Change in America, 1952–1990.* Atlanta, Ga.: Glenmary Research Center, 1994.

Maps for Pilgrims

Edney, Matthew. *Mapping an Empire: The Geographical Construction of British India, 1765–1843.* Chicago: University of Chicago Press, 1997.

Gole, Susan. *Indian Maps and Plans: From Earliest Times to the Advent of European Surveys.* New Delhi: Manohar, 1989.

Pieper, Jan. "A Pilgrim's Map of Benares: Notes on Codification in Hindu Cartography," *GeoJournal* 3 (1979): 215–18.

Schwartzberg, Joseph E. "Geographical Mapping," in J. B. Harley and David Woodward (eds.). *History of Cartography, Volume 2 Book 1: Cartography in Traditional Islamic and South Asian Societies.* Chicago: University of Chicago Press, 1992, pp. 388–493.

Varanasi Research Project—Visualized Space. Heidelberg: University of Heidelberg—South Asia Institute, 2001. http://benares.uni-hd.de

8

Agriculture

Vocabulary applied in this chapter
agricultural landscape
agricultural region
agricultural diffusion
environmental perception
Public Land Survey System
  (PLSS)
spatial zonation

New vocabulary
satellite imagery
resolution
wavelength
AVHRR
electromagnetic spectrum
infrared
Landsat TM
SPOT

⊕ 8.1
Agricultural Landscapes from Satellite Imagery

One way to monitor changes in **agricultural land use** and **landscape** pattern is through interpretation of satellite imagery. In this exercise, we will look at how satellite images can be used to explore different agricultural types and monitor or predict ecological change.

Types of Imagery

Unlike an air photo, which is a photograph taken with a camera and typically collected from an airplane, a **satellite image** is a digital image of some part of the earth's surface, collected by a sensor on a satellite. Satellite images differ by **resolution** and wavelength.

Each type of satellite image has its own resolution. The resolution of an image is comparable to the scale of a map: it defines the measure of detail of geographical information in the image.

For example, **Advanced Very High Resolution Radiometer (AVHRR)** images have a resolution of about a kilometer. This means that an object that measures one kilometer or more on earth will be visible in the image.

Landsat Thematic Mapper (Landsat TM) images have a resolution of 30 meters, meaning the images are made up of rectangles (or "pixels") 30 meters × 30 meters. This resolution comes out to a little less than a quarter of an acre. **SPOT** images, on the other hand, have a higher resolution of about 10 meters.

Like scale, resolution limits what kind of information can be shown. A farmer with one-acre fields, for example, would not find Landsat TM imagery useful because each field would be reduced to four pixels in the image, not enough to contain usable information. On the other hand, the same farmer might find Landsat TM imagery useful for understanding the agricultural patterns of the surrounding watershed or ecosystem.

Wavelength also influences the type of information that can be depicted in an image. Each satellite image is a picture of radiation from a particular part of the **electromagnetic spectrum**. Remote sensing scientists decide which part of the spectrum will be used in order to highlight certain features of the earth in the image.

For example, to map the spatial pattern of agriculture, geographers use satellite imagery from the **infrared** wavelength. Infrared allows image analysts to interpret the health and development of plants by measuring their chlorophyll reflectance levels.

Agricultural Systems in Border Landscapes

Study the two Landsat TM infrared images on the facing page. Both images depict parts of North Korea during August 2001.

In these images, the bright, reddish orange indicates paddy rice agriculture, darker orange indicates corn, yellow and green indicate other vegetation, and grey and white indicate urban areas. In the top image, you can see the orange of corn during harvest season in the vicinity of Pyongyang. In the bottom image, from coastal North Korea, paddy rice farming dominates the image.

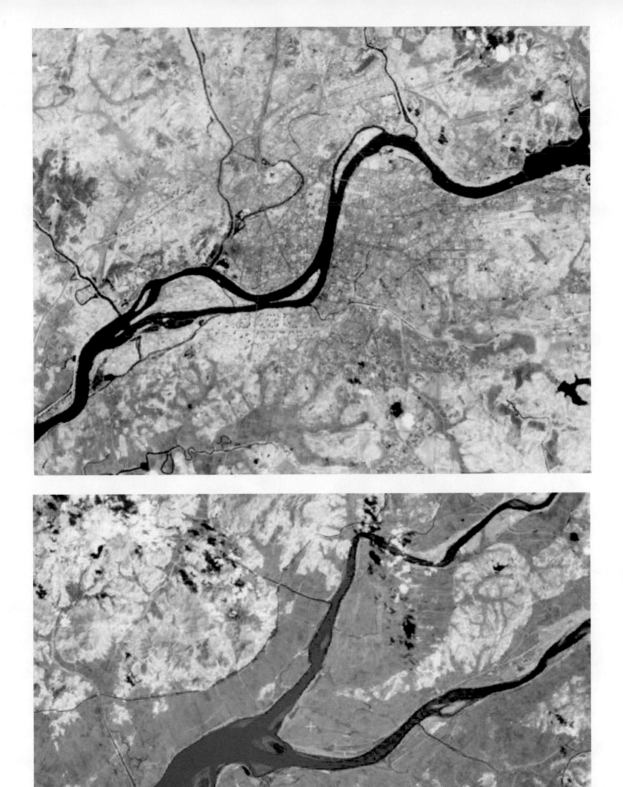

Landsat TM images, 2001 © USDA / Foreign Agricultural Service. Used with permission of USDA / FAS.

Landsat TM image - 20 Aug 98
USDA/FAS/PECAD

Landsat TM image, 1998 © USDA / Foreign Agricultural Service. Used with permission of USDA / FAS.

Satellite images can also be used to compare differences in agricultural practices between cultures, as in the next two Landsat TM infrared images. The above image shows the border of North Korea and China in August 1998.

Question 1: Reflect on the different types of agricultural systems that you have learned are characteristic of agricultural regions. What difference in agricultural systems between North Korea and China is depicted in the image?

NORTH and SOUTH KOREA

NORTH KOREA

SOUTH KOREA

LANDSAT TM 91/10/22
USDA/FAS

Landsat TM image, 1991 © USDA / Foreign Agricultural Service. Used with permission of USDA / FAS.

The image on this page shows the border between North and South Korea in October 1991. The coloring of this Landsat TM image is slightly different: unharvested paddy rice is depicted in white.

Question 2: What differences in agricultural systems between North and South Korea can you see in this image?

Monitoring Agricultural Conditions and Change

In 1997, North Korea suffered a devastating drought, the effects of which continue to influence North Koreans today.

The Foreign Agricultural Service (FAS, a division of the USDA) has been monitoring the agricultural conditions in North Korea in order to monitor, predict, and preempt such tragic consequences in the future. To make those kinds of predictions, the FAS relies on SPOT imagery.

Compare the two SPOT infrared images of Huanghae Province, below. Both images are from the month of August, in the years 1998 and 1997, respectively.

In these images, vegetation appears as red. The higher the levels of chlorophyll in the vegetation, the brighter the red of the image.

Question 3: What evidence can you find for the previous year's drought, as shown in the second image?

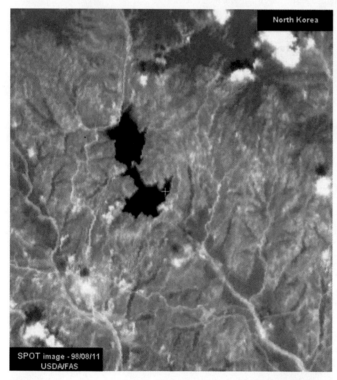

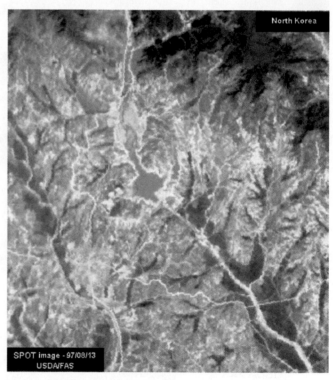

SPOT images, 1998, 1997 © USDA / Foreign Agricultural Service. Used with permission of USDA / FAS.

In this final infrared image from SPOT, the border between China and North Korea is shown for July 1997.

Question 4: What differences for the two countries can you see?

Question 5: How does a political border influence agricultural conditions during a drought?

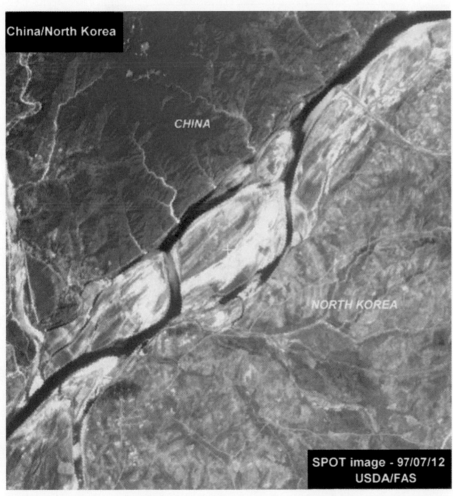

China/North Korea

CHINA

NORTH KOREA

SPOT image - 97/07/12
USDA/FAS

SPOT image, 1997 © USDA / Foreign Agricultural Service. Used with permission of USDA / FAS.

⊕ 8.2
Diffusion and Differentiation in Agricultural Regions

How does the geography of a crop change over time? How do you track agricultural diffusion cartographically?

This exercise utilizes the online mapping of the National Agricultural Statistics Service (also part of the USDA). The NASS Web site allows you to query historical data for major crops in the United States, both in terms of total acreage harvested and product yield per acre. The online maps at this site allow us to go beyond generalizations about major agricultural regions and deeper into the details about processes within and between those regions.

Step 1 Launch your browser and navigate to the "National Agricultural Statistics Service, Charts and Maps" link under Exercise 8.2 in the "Exploring Human Geography with Maps" section of the *Human Mosaic* Web site shown in the screenshot, top right.

Step 2 This will take you to a choropleth map for the most recent harvest, as in the bottom screenshot on this page.

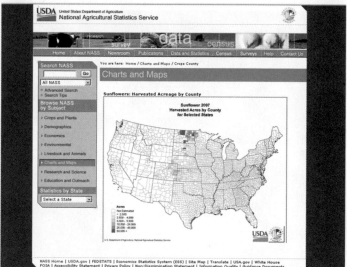

Screenshots from National Agricultural Statistics Service (NASS), U.S. Department of Agriculture Web site, 2009. Used with permission.

Question 1: Describe the regional distribution of the sunflower harvest. Where is the highest harvest centered? What are the boundaries of the sunflower-growing region?

Refrigeration and transport technologies have changed the influence of distance and seasons on agriculture. As a result, the spatial zones of agriculture that von Thünen observed have been altered. NASS includes data on the diffusion of an element in the "cool chains" for agricultural commodities, cold storage space.

Step 3   Move your cursor to the "You are here:" navigation line near the top of the page, and click on the "Charts and Maps" link. From the "Crops and Plants" list, select "Cold Storage, Crops."

Step 4   At the "Cold Storage" page, scroll down the page to the "Cold Storage—Space" subsection and click on the links for "Gross Refrigerated Space, 1923" and "Gross Refrigerated Space, 2005."

Question 2: Describe the changes in the availability and spatial distribution of cold storage space between 1923 and 2005.

Question 3: Given what you have learned thus far about symbolizing data on maps, what are some of the factors that make the colors and hatching symbols on these maps difficult to interpret?

The NASS data is also useful for tracking spatial zonation, specifically regional variations in agricultural productivity. Durum wheat, an essential ingredient in high-quality pasta, is an interesting crop to track graphically.

Step 5   Return to the "Charts and Maps" Web site and click on the link for "Wheat, Durham" in the right column. Compare the "Harvested Acreage by County" and the "Yield per Harvested Acre by County." For easier comparison, choose the PDF versions of each map because they open in separate windows.

Question 4: What, in general, is the difference between the acres planted in durum wheat in North Dakota versus Southern California? Which region has the highest number of acres planted in this crop?

Question 5: Compare your findings for harvest data to the information in the yield map. Which region has the highest yield of durum wheat?

Question 6: What do you think might be some factors contributing to the regional disparity between acres harvested and yield for this crop?

⏻ 8.3 Environmental Perception, Agriculturists, and the Map

Although maps have the power to alter our **perception** of agricultural regions and landscapes, that power is not always successfully interpreted and used by the map reader, or by society. A good example of this comes from a map by John Wesley Powell, former director of the United States Geological Survey (USGS).

In 1878, Powell presented the findings of his extensive research on the Great Basin in his work *Report on the Lands of the Arid Region of the United States.* Through written and cartographic narrative, Powell documented the arid nature of the West and warned against the popular perception that the Western environment could support large-scale agricultural expansion. Powell reported that expansion could proceed, but in order to preserve the agricultural health of the region, the federal government would have to proceed with specific, water-conscious measures.

"Arid Region of the United States Showing Drainage Districts," by John Wesley Powell. *USGS Eleventh Annual Report Part II—Irrigation*, Plate LXIX. Washington: GPO, 1891.

In particular, Powell hoped to convince the Department of the Interior that the settlement of the West would be sustainable only if political jurisdictions within the states were based on watershed boundaries, rather than the arbitrary gridded lines of the **Public Land Survey System** (PLSS). Powell perceived that watersheds would best be preserved if neighbors with common interests cared for the watersheds at the community level. With communities built on the arbitrary grid of the PLSS, those watersheds would be divided across many counties.

Two years later, in a follow-up report, Powell illustrated his ideas in a detailed map, titled "Arid Region of the United States Showing Drainage Districts," shown on page 116. In the map, he graphically demonstrated that political districts created by watershed boundaries would organize the region into manageable units.

In this case, the map failed to alter the environmental perception of agriculturists. Powell's watershed district proposal was ignored by the Department of Interior, and Powell resigned from his position as Director of the USGS two years after the publication of 1891 report. Perception of the West as a region of agricultural expansion and opportunity continued to pervade the American imagination, and counties and agricultural property boundaries were based on the grid of the PLSS as planned.

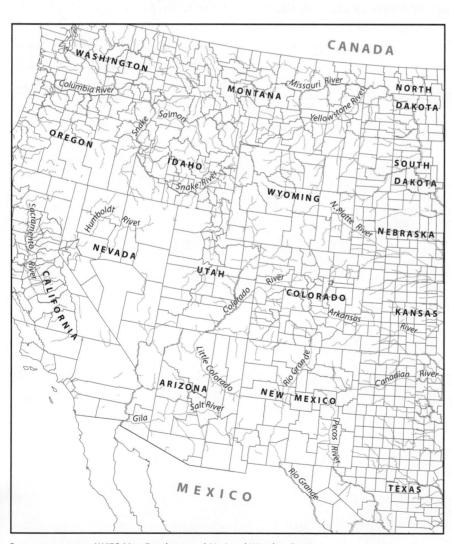

Base map source: AWIPS Map Database and National Weather Service.

Question 1: Compare Powell's map to the present-day county boundaries and rivers in the map on the left. Are there any counties that follow parts of the watershed? If so, in which states?

Question 2: Imagine that Powell's ideas had been implemented and Western jurisdiction was based on the watershed unit rather than the county unit. Which state do you think would be most different today and why?

Question 3: What do you think the overall agricultural impact would have been if Powell's jurisdictions had been implemented?

Question 4: Do you think there would be drawbacks to Powell's plan? Explain your reasoning why or why not.

Question 5: What factors determine whether a map successfully alters public consciousness about a geographical theme?

Sources and Suggested Readings

Satellite Imagery

Lillesand, Thomas M., Ralph W. Kiefer, and Jonathan W. Chipman. *Remote Sensing and Image Interpretation.* 6th ed. N.Y.: Wiley, 2007.

U.S. Geological Survey. *Earthshots: Satellite Images of Environmental Change.* 14 Aug. 2008. <http://earthshots.usgs.gov/tableofcontents>

Agricultural Diffusion

Hunt, R. Douglas. *American Agriculture: A Brief History.* Revised ed. West Lafayette, Indiana: Purdue University Press, 2002.

Pillsbury, Richard. *No Foreign Food: The American Diet in Time and Place.* Colorado: Westfield Press, 1998.

Shortridge, Barbara G. and James R. Shortridge, eds. *The Taste of American Place: A Reader on Regional and Ethnic Foods.* New York: Rowman and Littlefield, 1998.

John Wesley Powell

Powell, John Wesley. "Arid Region of the United States Showing Drainage Districts." *United States Geological Survey, Eleventh Annual Report, 1889–90: Part II, Irrigation Survey.* Washington, D.C.: Government Printing Office, 1891.

Powell, John Wesley. *Report on the Lands of the Arid Region.* Washington, D.C.: Government Printing Office, 1878.

Stegner, Wallace. *Beyond the Hundredth Meridian: John Wesley Powell and the Second Opening of the West.* N.Y.: Penguin, 1992.

CHAPTER

9

Industry

Vocabulary applied in this chapter
industrial regions:
   formal, functional,
   vernacular
technopole
industrial landscape
industry types:
   primary
   secondary
   service sector

New vocabulary
Geographic Information
   Systems (GIS)
Web GIS

✵ ⊕ 9.1
Exploring the Industrial Infrastructure

This exercise explores the geography of service industries. How are service industries located in relationship to each other in the city? What is the infrastructure that supports them? To understand their we will use the capabilities of GIS.

Introduction to GIS

When mapping combines the analytical capabilities of the computer with the visualization benefits of the map, this is known as a **Geographic Information System** or **GIS.** A GIS consists of a computer, the software tools for performing GIS analysis, digital databases, and database analysis. Though people often print paper maps in order to display the results of their analysis, the greater strength of a GIS lies in the computer system itself, where the user can graphically examine different views of a spatial data set as a means of developing a deeper knowledge of that data than afforded by nongraphic devices such as tables or descriptive statistics.

Geographers use GIS for any kind of work in which the primary goal is to store, analyze, and graphically view spatial databases. A GIS is more useful than a paper map when you have data associated with each of the geographical features of a particular place and you wish to perform statistical analyses of this feature data. The applications for GIS are wide-ranging and are used throughout physical and human geographical research, limited only by the availability (and quality) of data for a particular place.

When GIS is combined with the interactive capabilities of the Web, it is known as **Web GIS.** Web GIS has grown increasingly popular in recent years as an effective means of providing geographical data in an accessible format. Whereas a conventional GIS demands that a user have special software in order to access its geographical databases, software that typically requires special training for use, a Web GIS by contrast can be accessed with nothing more complicated than a Web browser. For this reason, it is ideally suited to the dissemination of data for geographical query to a wide range of users.

In Salt Lake City, the Engineering Division of Salt Lake City Public Services hosts a publicly available Web GIS.

Step 1 Launch your browser and navigate to the "Salt Lake City GIS" link under Exercise 9.1 in the "Exploring Human Geography with Maps" section of the *Human Mosaic* Web site. This will take you to the table of contents for the Salt Lake City online map server, shown here.

Step 2 In the main section, under Available Maps: Map Name, click "Zoning." This will launch a second window with the Web GIS application.

Screenshot from Salt Lake City GIS Web site, 2009. Used with permission.

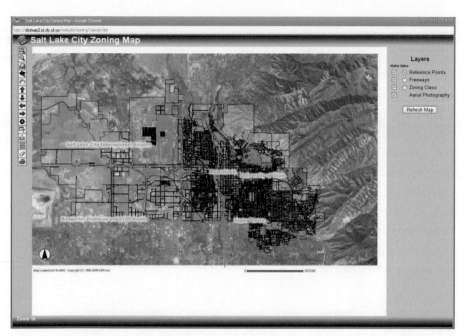

Screenshot from Salt Lake City GIS Web site, 2009. Used with permission.

I, Institutional
M-1, Light Manufacturing
M-2, Heavy Manufacturing
MH, Mobile Home Park
MU, Mixed Use
OS, Open Space
PL, Public Lands
PL2, Public Lands (Library)
R-1-12000, Single Family Residential
R-1-5000, Single Family Residential
R-1-7000, Single Family Residential
R-2, Single and Two Family Residential
R-MU, Residential/Mixed Use
RB, Residential/Business
RMF-30, Low Density Multifamily Residential
RMF-35, Moderate Density Multifamily
   Residential
RMF-45, Moderate/High Density Multifamily
   Residential
RMF-75, High Density Multifamily Residential
RO, Residential Office
RP, Research Park
SR-1, Special Development Pattern Residential
SR-3, Special Development Pattern Residential
UI, Urban Institutional

Step 3 Take a few moments to get oriented with this interactive map, shown above. On the left, a toolbar provides tools for zooming and panning, directional moves, identify and measure queries, and printing. The selected tool is outlined in red and described in the bottom left corner of the map. The view should be set to its default tool setting with the "Zoom In" tool selected in red and indicated at the bottom left.

Directly below the main map, a scale bar indicates distance at this particular view of the city.

On the right side of the map, the data layers available for this view are listed. Some data layers are available at only certain scales, so this list will change when you zoom in and out of the map.

Step 4 In the "Layers" list, click the radio button next to the "Zoning Class" layer to make it

active. By activating it, you have now made this layer available for query from the database associated with the features on that layer.

Step 5 Try out the query by first clicking on the "Identify" tool in the tool bar, then clicking on any color block in the map. Below the map, you will see a return line with a "Zoning Class" identified. The meanings of these codes are as follows:

AG, Agriculture
AG-2, Agriculture-2 Acre Minimum
AG-5, Agriculture-5 Acre Minimum
AG-20, Agriculture-20 Acre Minimum
AIRPORT, Airport
BP, Business Park
C-SHBD, Sugar House Business
CB, Community Business
CC, Commercial Corridor
CG, General Commercial
CN, Neighborhood Commercial
CS, Community Shopping
D-1, Central Business District
D-2, Downtown Support District
D-3, Downtown Warehouse District
D-4, Secondary Central Business District
EI, Extractive Industry
FP, Foothills Protection
FR-1, FR-1/43560 Foothills Estates Residential
FR-2, FR-2/21780 Foothills Residential
FR-3, FR-3/12000 Foothills Residential
GMU, Gateway Mixed Use

Step 6 Review what you have already learned about **primary** and **secondary industries** and **services.** With the table of zoning class codes as a guide, use your query tool to explore the relative locations of these economic activity categories.

Question 1: In general, how are these categories located in Salt Lake City? Use the district names, called "Reference Points" in the "Layers" list, as a reference.

Step 7 With the "Zoom In" tool selected, click your cursor on the main map until you are zoomed in on the center and eastern portions of Salt Lake City, at about the scale as shown in the top figure on page 122. You can use the "Pan" tool to adjust the way the map is centered in the frame.

Step 8   In the "Layers" list, uncheck the "Visible" box for Aerial Photography, and then click "Refresh Map." This will return a map of highways and zoning regions only, as at the bottom of this page.

As you have also learned, service industries can be categorized as producer services, consumer services, and transportation or communication services.

Question 2: Review what you know about the kinds of industries associated with these three types. Which of the zoning class codes seem to be clearly associated with each type? Make a list of the codes strongly associated with producer, consumer, and transportation/communication services.

With this list, you can map the detailed geography of service industries as they are embedded in the urban landscape of Salt Lake City.

Step 9   Zoom in to a larger scale, and you will see the zoning class codes activated in the map itself, as shown on the facing page. You can see that the hues in the map are associated with specific types of zoning class codes to facilitate our interpretation of where the different types of zoning begin and end with respect to city blocks.

Step 10   Now, using your "Zoom," "Pan," and "Query" tools, begin assembling your custom service industry map of Salt Lake City, using the base map provided on the opposite page. For each of the three types, fill the blocks according to your own area symbolization in the legend. You can use either three separate colors or three separate line patterns, depending on your preference.

Question 3: Evaluate the geography you have just visualized through area symbolization. What do you see? Describe the shape of each type of industry. Is it contiguous or noncontiguous? Where is the center or node for each?

Question 4: How are these three types of service industries interrelated in space?

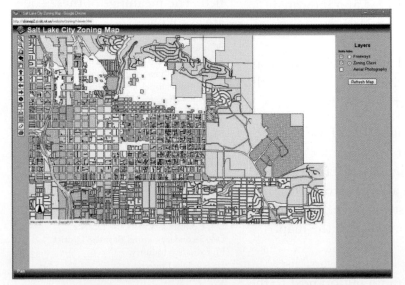

Screenshots from Salt Lake City GIS Web site, 2009. Used with permission.

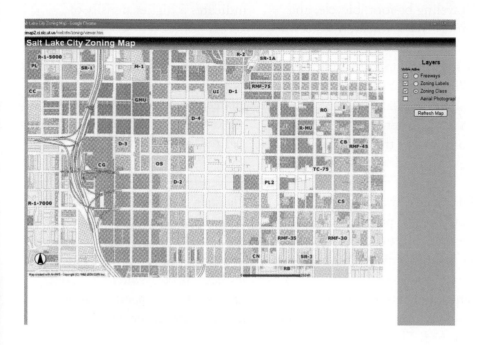

☐ producer services
☐ consumer services
☐ transportation/
    communication services

Visualizing ephemeral infrastructures

Although GIS has been fundamental to the implementation of centralized spatial databases such as Salt Lake City GIS, it can also be a powerful tool for analyzing decentralized and ephemeral data. In this section we turn to the use of GIS for mapping a particularly ephemeral service industry, the geography of Wi-Fi networks.

Like radio, Wi-Fi makes use of dedicated airwaves in the electromagnetic spectrum for transmitting information, but in analog to digital format. A community with a healthy Wi-Fi presence is one which offers a rich environment for digital networking between

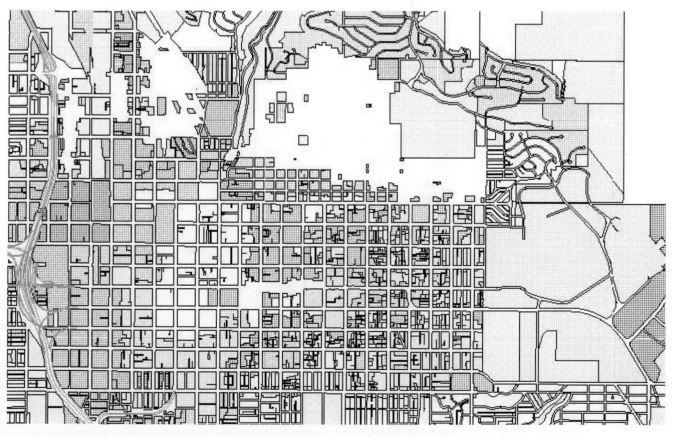

Screenshots from Salt Lake City GIS Web site, 2009. Used with permission.

laptops, hand-held devices, and desktop computers.

Recognizing that investment in Wi-Fi both attracts new businesses and supports the growth of existing industries, some cities have invested in city-wide Wi-Fi networks as part of their municipal services commitment. In most places, however, the Wi-Fi infrastructure is accidental, the result of hundreds of localized networks, private or publicly owned, overlapping in space. Wi-Fi geography thus remains a decentralized, often invisible, and highly ephemeral landscape, an uneven surface of varying signal strengths and access densities.

In his Geosimulation Lab, the geographer Paul Torrens is working on the question of how to visualize Wi-Fi geographies in in order to better understand their influence on industrial location and growth. Torrens focuses on Salt Lake City because it ranks high in terms of overall personal home computer use, and it has no centralized, municipal Wi-Fi network in place.

Traveling by foot, bicycle, and car, Torrens' research team traversed Salt Lake City's central districts, sampling and measuring Wi-Fi access points and signals.

In a Wi-Fi network, an access point marks the location of any device broadcasting a Wi-Fi signal. In an area of about ten square kilometers, they found 1,739 Wi-Fi access points, on both secured and unsecured networks, by sampling over 500,000 signals.

These points were then downloaded into a GIS database and mapped. Through GIS analysis, they converted these points to a continuous surface in order to visualize the change in access point density through the city, as shown in the map below.

In this map of access point density, the height of the red surface indicates a higher density of access points. The colors in the street map below correspond with the team's own categorization of industrial districts in the city center, as summarized in the overall districts map on the right.

Question 5: Using the overall districts map as a guide, describe the pattern of access that you see in the density surface map. In which districts are the greatest and fewest number of access points? Is there a district where the access is particularly sparse?

Question 6: Compare these access densities to your own map of service industry types in this city. Which types of services seem to be generating the highest number of access points?

Map ©2008 Paul M. Torrens. In Torrens, Paul M.: Wi-Fi Geographies. *Annals of the Association of American Geographers* 98(1), 2008 p. 73 (Figure 5).

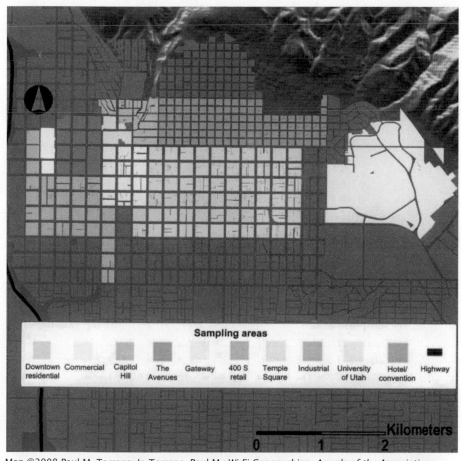

Map ©2008 Paul M. Torrens. In Torrens, Paul M.: Wi-Fi Geographies. *Annals of the Association of American Geographers* 98(1), 2008 p. 67 (Figure 3).

Sampling areas

Downtown residential · Commercial · Capitol Hill · The Avenues · Gateway · 400 S retail · Temple Square · Industrial · University of Utah · Hotel/convention · Highway

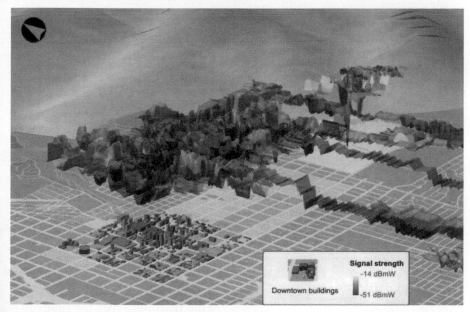

Downtown buildings

Signal strength
-14 dBmW
-51 dBmW

Map ©2008 Paul M. Torrens. In Torrens, Paul M.: Wi-Fi Geographies. *Annals of the Association of American Geographers* 98(1), 2008 p. 76 (Figure 8).

Torrens' team then re-mapped their data set with a focus on signal strength, to generate a visual surface of the pattern of Wi-Fi signal strengths through the city, as shown below left.

At this scale, it is difficult to see the correlation between signal strength and access density. Torrens' team found, however, that the high signal strengths do not necessarily correspond to the same places where there are a high number of access points. A high density of Wi-Fi access points, they found, can degrade signal strength when all access points are competing for the same radio frequencies.

Question 7: Based on what you can see in these surface maps, which districts in Salt Lake City seem to offer the strongest Wi-Fi infrastructure support to producer and consumer services?

🔍 9.2
Industry and the Environment on the Web

As you saw in the previous exercise, Web GIS is useful for revealing industrial regions. It can also be useful for revealing the impact of industry on the environment. The Environmental Protection Agency (EPA) uses Web GIS as one of several modes for disseminating environmental information to the general public. Its interactive Web site, "EnviroMapper," was created as a resource for citizens to make geographical comparisons between the physical context of their communities and the EPA-regulated industries located there.

Step 1   Launch your browser and navigate to the "EnviroMapper" link under Exercise 9.2 in the "Exploring Human Geography with Maps" section of the *Human Mosaic* Web site.

You will see the "EnviroMapper for EnviroFacts" front page as in the image above right. This is the geographic gateway to using the EPA's interactive data browser.

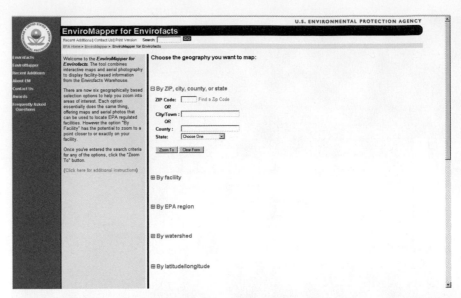

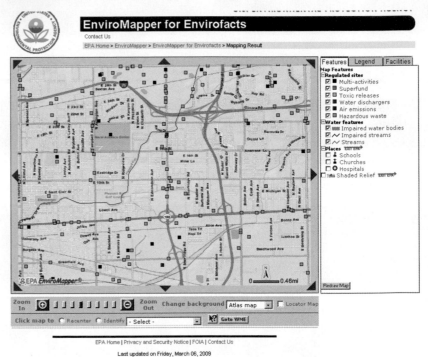

Screenshots courtesy of the U.S. EPA Office of Environmental Information. Used with permission.

Step 2   In the search boxes on the right, type the name or Zip Code for your hometown, and then click on "Zoom To." If you do not live in a place included in the EPA database, search for another town you know. This will return a zoomed map of this area code, with streets, highways, and water features indicated, as in the bottom image on this page.

To the right of the map, the legend column lists the map layers that can be turned on and off in the region you have chosen. Bold headings ("Regulated sites," "Places," "Water features," "Political boundaries," and "Flood zones") indicate that an additional list of mappable features exists for that category. To view additional data layers, click on the "plus" signs to the left of the headings.

Step 3 Experiment with the data layers by exploring the layers listed under "Regulated sites." Click on the boxes next to "Superfund," "Toxic releases," "Water dischargers," "Air emissions," and "Hazardous waste," and then click on the "Redraw Map" button at the top of the legend.

Question 1: Make a list showing how many of each EPA site type exist in your zip code area:

Type
Number

Superfund clean-up sites
Toxic releases
Water dischargers
Air emissions
Hazardous waste

Question 2: Look at the distribution of the EPA regulated sites. How are they clustered? Using your knowledge of this place, describe the distribution of these sites with respect to the physical and built landscape of your town or city. Zoom in and out as necessary to assist you with your interpretation.

Step 4 You can identify any of the regulated sites by name at EnviroMapper. Click the "Show Site Info" radio button in the blue field below the map; if this radio button is not showing, zoom in and it will appear. Now, hover your cursor over a feature symbol on the map and its name will appear. Clicking on the symbol will redirect you to an EPA site report. Alternately, you can select the "Facilities" tab at the top of the legend box and scroll through a list of regulated sites.

Another layer of interpretation can be added by exploring the relationship among the EPA regulated sites, water features, and places.

Step 5 If you have not done so already, turn on the "Water features" and "Places" symbols by clicking on the "plus" signs to the left of the headings and then clicking in the check boxes. Click on the "Redraw Map" button once the water features and places have been chosen.

In order to identify "Water features" and "Places," click the "Identify" radio button below the map, and in the "Select" dropdown menu, choose the feature category you would like to identify. Next, click on that feature symbol in the map. EnviroMapper will return the name or names associated with that symbol, with a link to more information below the map.

Question 3: How are the EPA regulated sites clustered with respect to populated places, surrounding schools, churches, and hospitals?

Question 4: Are there certain types of emitters that exist apart from these populated areas?

Question 5: Do sites exist on or around water features? If so, have the water features been identified by the EPA as "impaired"? Are there cases where a regulated site and an unimpaired water feature coincide?

The map provides a good picture of the types of EPA sites and their location relative to water and populated places—but how does this relate to the major types of industrial activity?

Step 6 Open a new browser window and navigate to the "EPA My Environment" link under Exercise 9.2 in the "Exploring Human Geography with Maps" section of the *Human Mosaic* Web site. Doing so will take you to the MyEnvironment homepage, shown here.

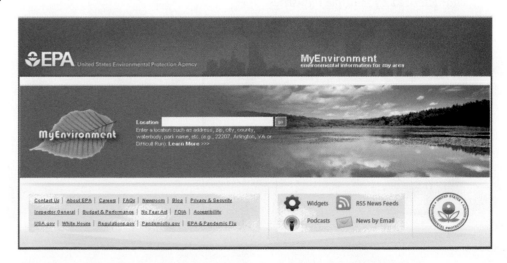

Step 7 In the "Location" box, type the name or Zip Code for your chosen place, and then click on "Go." This will return a zoomed map of your place, with streets, water features, and EPA-monitored sites indicated by industry, as in the bottom image on this page.

You can identify sites reporting to the EPA by placing your cursor over the site markers on the map. Clicking on the name of the site will take you to detailed information about its environmental impact, including a Toxic Release Inventory. To the right of the map, the legend lists sites by the type of industry (primary, secondary, or service). You can turn on and off types of industries with the radio buttons in the legend.

Step 8 Using the radio buttons and your cursor, browse the sites on the map associated with each industry, noting any clusters of types of industry.

Question 6: Did you find any industry specific clusters? Are some locations characterized by multiple industries?

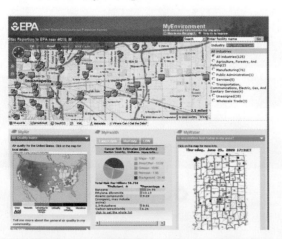

Question 7: Examine your results from Question 3 above. Do these results change your perception of the environmental impact of industries in your town? If so, how?

Step 9 Launch your browser and navigate to the "TRI Explorer" link under Exercise 9.2 in the "Exploring Human Geography with Maps" section of the *Human Mosaic* Web site.

Step 10 In the "Geographic Location" dropdown menu, select "Enter a ZIP Code" and then enter your Zip code in the field. Leave the default Year of Data set to 2007, and click "Generate Report." (If no data is reported for your region in this year, try an earlier date such as 1999 or 2001 for your report.)

Question 8: What are the top three chemicals released on-site in your town? Off-site?

● 9.3
Exploring the Industrial Locations of the Past

One way to calculate fire insurance for urban areas is through extensive mapping of the building materials and urban context of every building. From the 1920s to the 1960s, fire insurance mapping in the United States was dominated by the Sanborn Map Company. Sanborn maps can be found for every city in the country.

Once used to calculate fire risk and changes in fire risk over time, Sanborn maps today are a gold mine of information about changes in the urban landscape. Highly detailed and large scale, the maps are sources for the names of building owners and the locations of businesses and residences over time. They also document the vanished, ancient, urban landscape, such as the paths of trolley and rail beds, the locations of stables, mill races, and even outdoor toilets.

Today these maps can be found in the archives of university libraries, city archives, and research libraries. At the University of Virginia, the Sanborn maps of Charlottesville, Virginia, are freely available online through the resources of the Geospatial & Statistical Data Center. This exercise utilizes the Charlottesville Sanborns as tools for interpreting the historical **industrial landscape.**

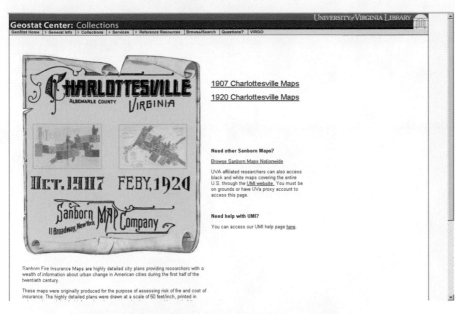

Screenshot, © Geospatial and Statistical Data Center, University of Virginia Library Web site (http://fisher.lib.virginia.edu), 2009. Used with permission.

Step 1   Launch your browser and navigate to the "Sanborn Fire Insurance Maps" link under Exercise 9.3 in the "Exploring Human Geography with Maps" section of the *Human Mosaic* Web site.

Step 2   From the right-hand column, click on "1920 Charlottesville Maps." Then click on "Symbols" from the horizontal navigation bar near the top of the page. This link takes you to a brief visual guide to interpreting the symbols and color coding of the Sanborn Maps, as in the screenshot to the left, bottom. Review the guide and study the explanation of symbols.

Question 1: Why did the Sanborn company map only parts of the city, rather than the city as a whole?

Question 2: How do you think this will limit interpretation of the cultural geography of industrial location in Charlottesville?

Skylights, windows, fire escapes, the thickness of walls, garages, elevators, sprinkler systems, asbestos shingles, and building height are all commonly noted on building drawings as well.

a fire escape   skylights   a fire door

Buildings are also labeled as to their function. Civic or prominent buildings like schools, theatres, churches, businesses and offices are often named on Sanborn Maps. For those not named outright, the letter D indicates a dwelling, F a flat, S a store, and A an auto garage. Often notes like "Apts" for apartments will also appear.

a dwelling

A variety of more specific notations often appear in drawings as well, most pertaining to facts that would pertain to a buildings tolerance to fire, as these maps were intended for use by fire insurance companies first and foremost.

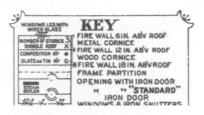

Screenshot, © Geospatial and Statistical Data Center, University of Virginia Library Web site (http://fisher.lib.virginia.edu), 2009. Used with permission.

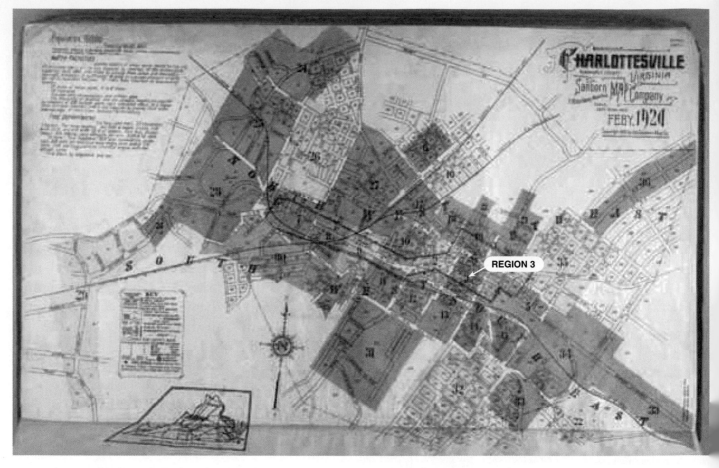

Screenshot, © Geospatial and Statistical Data Center, University of Virginia Library Web site (http://fisher.lib.virginia.edu), 2009. Used with permission.

Step 3 On the "How to" page, scroll to the top and click "1920" or use the browser's back function to return to the home page for the 1920 Charlottesville map.

Step 4 Click on the link for the "Original Sanborn Index Map" to view a clickable map index of the city.

The full-size version will not fit on your monitor, so to help you navigate, a small version of the index is reproduced above.

Using the index, you can link to the individual, detailed sheet maps of the city.

Step 5 Navigate to the downtown region of Charlottesville, an area depicted in pink on the index, where Main and Market streets parallel each other. This is labeled region "3."

Step 6 Click on the "3" to link from the index to Sheet 3, the detailed map for that region, via the Sheet 3 menu.

You should now be at a page that looks like the screenshot on page 131 .

Step 7 To begin exploring the industrial activity of downtown Charlottesville, click on the "Download Map" link. Depending on the speed of your Internet connection, this image will take some time to download.

Step 8 Right click on the downloaded file folder and extract the zipped files. Navigate your way into the file folder and click on the TIF image of downtown. The resolution of the JPEG image is too low for your analysis.

Step 9 Zoom into E. Main Street, which runs horizontally across the bottom of the image.

Question 3: What kinds of industries exist on E. Main Street? To answer this question, use the vocabulary for classifying industrial activity (primary, secondary, and service) that you have learned from your textbook.

Question 4: In what types of buildings were these services located? (If you cannot remember the codes used in the Sanborn maps, you can reread the symbol explanation any time by clicking on the "Symbols" link at the top or bottom of the page.)

Now begin exploring northward by scrolling slowly upward on the map.

Question 5: How does industrial activity change as one travels away from E. Main Street?

Question 6: Using the mapped information about building size and type, and comparing the lot sizes, how do you think the cultural landscape is changing?

Question 7: What is the difference in industrial activity between the neighborhood north of E. Main Street (along Market Street) and the neighborhood south of E. Main Street (along Water Street)?

Question 8: How does the railroad alter the industrial geography of the city?

Screenshot, © Geospatial and Statistical Data Center, University of Virginia Library Web site (http://fisher.lib.virginia.edu), 2009. Used with permission.

Step 10 Return to the Web site and look again at the map index. You can zoom in to get a more detailed view of the city.

Question 9: Imagine that you are a traveler on the Chesapeake & Ohio Railroad. You can see on the index that the Chesapeake & Ohio line enters the city of Charlottesville from the northwest corner and exits to the southeast.

It is 1920, and you are traveling east. Charlottesville is not your destination, only a city that you are traveling through. As the train runs slowly through the city, you get a clear view of the city from your window on the south side of the train.

What do you see?

Describe the changes in the industrial landscape as you travel through Charlottesville. Use the index to guide you to the detailed sheet maps through which the Chesapeake & Ohio tracks run.

Sources and Suggested Readings

Geographic Information Systems

Goodchild, Michael F. "Geographic Information Systems," in Susan Hanson (ed.). *Ten Geographic Ideas That Changed the World.* New Brunswick, N.J.: Rutgers University Press, 1997, pp. 60–83.

Fire Insurance Maps

Oswald, Diane L. *Fire Insurance Maps: Their History and Applications.* College Station, Tex.: Lacewing Press, 1997.

Karrow, Robert, and Ronald E. Grim. "Two Examples of Thematic Maps: Civil War and Fire Insurance Maps," in David Buisseret (ed.). *From Sea Charts to Satellite Images: Interpreting North American History through Maps.* Chicago: University of Chicago Press, 1990, pp. 213–237.

Wi-Fi Geography

Torrens, Paul M. 2008. Wi-Fi geographies. *Annals of the Association of American Geographers* 98(1):59–84.

Zook, Matthew. *The Geography of the Internet Industry: Venture Capital, Dot-coms, and Local Knowledge.* Malden, Mass: Blackwell Publishing, 2005.

CHAPTER
10

Urbanization

Vocabulary applied in this chapter
urbanization
site and situation
urban sprawl
urban morphology
urban landscape

New vocabulary
remote sensing
MODIS
true-color imagery
false-color imagery
LIDAR
pixel
overlay

✦ 10.1
Urbanization and Natural Hazards

Remote sensing is the use of any type of geographic imagery—including photography, radar, sonar, and satellite imagery—to interpret, measure, analyze, and map geographical information. In Chapter 8, for example, you explored two types of remote sensing, Landsat and SPOT satellite imagery, and examined their use for monitoring agricultural land use change.

As different types of imagery will yield different kinds of information about a geographical situation, researchers often blend imagery sources in order to gain a more complex, multi-scaled analysis of a particular place. This approach is particularly useful for interpreting the impact of natural hazards on urbanization because such impacts occur at different scales and may affect water resources, vegetation, soils, and built infrastructure, each of which is best served by a different type of imagery. In this exercise, we will explore how remote sensing has been used to understand Hurricane Katrina, both in the analysis of the storm's impacts as well as in the ongoing negotiations of rebuilding the city of New Orleans.

New Orleans Imagery Across Scales and Sensors

To start, let's look at a small scale image of the Mississippi Delta region as a whole. The image below was recorded on March 5, 2001 by the **Moderate Resolution Imaging Spectroradiometer (MODIS)** instrument onboard the NASA satellite Terra. Terra crosses the equator each morning; its twin satellite, Aqua, crosses the equator each evening. Through the combination of the two satellites, the entire earth is reimaged every two days. MODIS imagery is used to monitor multiple dimensions of geographical information related to global change, including changes to land cover, ocean color, and atmospheric properties.

This is a **true color image,** meaning that the colors are designed to appear the same color as they would if we were to perceive them with human eyes. (The opposite of true-color is **false-color imagery,** which represents geographical data using unnatural colors in order to highlight aspects of those features. In Exercise 8.1, for example, you analyzed false-color Landsat imagery in order to detect changes in vegetation type on the ground.) This image reveals that it was taken shortly after rain because we can see brown sediment from the Mississippi River flow into the Gulf of Mexico.

Image courtesy Liam Gumley, Space Science and Engineering Center, University of Wisconsin-Madison and the MODIS Science team. NASA Visible Earth (visibleearth.nasa.gov/view_rec.php?id=1650).

Question 1: Recall what you have learned from your text about the site and situation of New Orleans, and compare these concepts to the MODIS image. Which aspects of the city's site and situation can be seen in the satellite image?

Image courtesy of the USGS Center for Earth Resources Observation & Science (CEROS).

Hurricane Katrina made its first landfall in Florida on August 23, 2005 as a Category 1 storm; when it made a second landfall on August 29, passing New Orleans, it was a Category 3.

In the two Landsat images, above right, the city of New Orleans is shown as it appeared first on April 24, and second on August 30, the day after the second landfall. In the later image, the dark blue floodwaters can be seen submerging the city south of Lake Pontchartrain.

Compare these images to the demographic map, below right. This map shows median household income, by block group, from Census 2000.

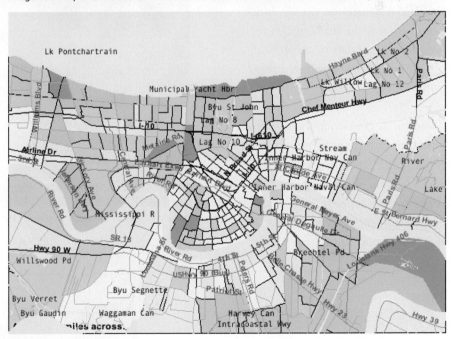

Data Classes

Dollars

	0 - 23293
	23390 - 34250
	34375 - 47695
	47928 - 72403
	73229 - 150487

Screenshot from the U.S. Census Bureau Web site, American FactFinder (http://factfinder.census.gov), 2009.

Question 2: Compare the standing water in the Landsat image to neighborhood income levels in the map. From the proportion of the city visible behind the cloud cover, can you interpret on whom the storm is having the greatest immediate impacts?

The next two Landsat images document the city eight days later, on September 7, and sixteen days later, on September 15. In both images, the dark shades of the flood waters can be seen still engulfing the city streets before being pumped back into Lake Pontchartrain to the north.

Question 3: Looking again at the median income map, which neighborhoods continue to be submerged one and two weeks later?

Question 4: In your reading of the map below of number of applicants for FEMA assistance, also by block group, what is the relationship between the number of assistance applicants, income level, and floodwater inundation?

Question 5: Now compare the assistance applicants to the map of number of people with flood insurance, by zip code area, on the opposite page. What is the relationship, if any, between insured residents and number of FEMA assistance applicants?

Image courtesy of the USGS Center for Earth Resources Observation & Science (CEROS).

FEMA Individual Assistance*
Katrina
(as of 3/16/06)

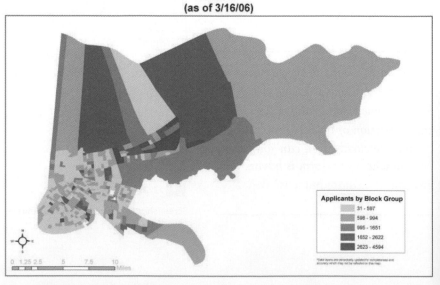

Applicants by Block Group
31 - 597
598 - 994
995 - 1651
1652 - 2622
2623 - 4594

Data distributed by LSU GIS Information Clearinghouse: CADGIS Research Lab, Louisiana State University, Baton Rouge, LA. 2005/2006 (http://www.katrina.lsu.edu).

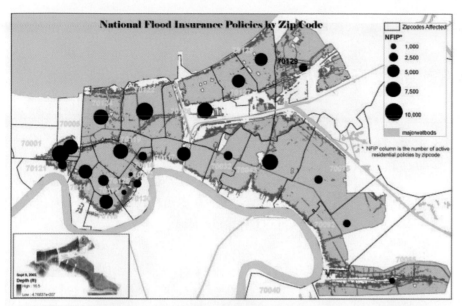

Data distributed by LSU GIS Information Clearinghouse: CADGIS Research Lab, Louisiana State University, Baton Rouge, LA. 2005/2006 (http://www.katrina.lsu.edu).

Blending Landsat and LIDAR

Another type of remote sensing technology, one used to measure elevations of objects, is known as **Light Detection and Ranging (LIDAR).** LIDAR imagery is produced by instruments flown on aircraft rather than satellites. Elevation is measured by the length of time for a laser beam to reflect back to the aircraft from the land or water surface below.

The LIDAR image below, for example, depicts the topography of New Orleans from a 2002 LIDAR survey.

Question 6: Compare the elevations of the LIDAR image to the maps of income and insurance. Which areas of the city seem most at risk for flooding in the event of a hurricane?

Question 7: Which areas of the city seem most at risk, financially, in the event of a hurricane?

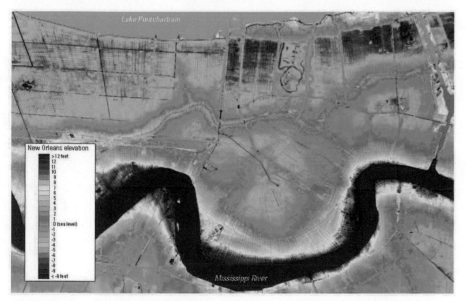

LIDAR image from Dean Gesch, Topography-based Analysis of Hurrican Katrina Inundation of New Orleans. *Science and the Storms: the USGS Response to the Hurricanes of 2005,* USGS Circular 1306, p. 54 (Figure 1).

A month after Katrina, U.S. Geological Survey scientists Robert Kayen and Brian Collins conducted a LIDAR survey of New Orleans to analyze the impacts of the levee breaches on the city. Beginning with the elevation data, they estimated the probable water depths from the storm and represented the data as an overlay on a Landsat false-color satellite image. In this map, the LIDAR and Landsat data are combined with locational data for the breached levee.

Question 8: Note the locations of the levee breaches in the LIDAR and Landsat overlay. Which neighborhoods of the city were most impacted by breaching? Were these the neighborhoods already potential flood or financial risks?

Question 9: How did the levee breaches change the storm's impact for the people of New Orleans?

LIDAR-survey site number	Location	Number of LIDAR scans
1	17th Street Canal	20
2	London Ave. Canal, North on east side	29 with Site 3
3	London Ave. Canal, North on west side	29 with Site 2
4	IHNC East Side, South Breach 9th ward	13
5	IHNC East Side, North Breach 9th ward	14
6	Lakeside Airport Levee Transition Breach	14 with Site 7
7	Lakeside Airport Levee I-Wall	14 with Site 6
8	Structural Distressed I-Wall at Container Wharf	20
9	Incipient Earth Levee failure	14
10	Entergy Plant I-Wall Scour	20

⊕ 10.2
Urbanization and Sprawl

As you learned in your textbook, although the world is becoming increasingly urbanized, different countries have different proportions of their populations residing in urban areas. The proportion of urbanized population in any one country influences the degree to which that country is affected by **urban sprawl.**

In Exercise 3.2, you explored tools for measuring the geography of sprawl at the metropolitan level in the United States. But how can sprawl be measured at the regional or continental level?

The difficulty of mapping urban sprawl at a regional or continental level has been an ongoing issue for geographers. Landsat TM, AVHRR, and SPOT imagery (see Chapter 8) are useful for interpretation of regional trends in land cover, but not necessarily for interpretation of differences between the built and nonbuilt environments.

In part, this is due to the scale problem: Landsat TM and AVHRR imagery do not offer the level of resolution necessary for classifying rural vs. urban areas. The higher resolutions of SPOT and other imagery sources can be used to map and monitor land transformations at the local level, but the large file sizes for such detailed digital imagery make it all but impossible to work outward to regional, much less global, land cover interpretation.

In 2001, scientists at NASA Goddard Space Flight Center, under the direction of biologist Marc Imhoff, created a global satellite image that shows the locations of light on the surface of the earth. As you can see in the image on page 140, the clustering of light shows the density and intensity of urbanization.

"Global City Lights" image by Robert Simmon and Craig Mayhew, Distributed Active Archive Center (DAAC), Goddard Space Flight Center, 2000. Used with permission of Robert Simmon.

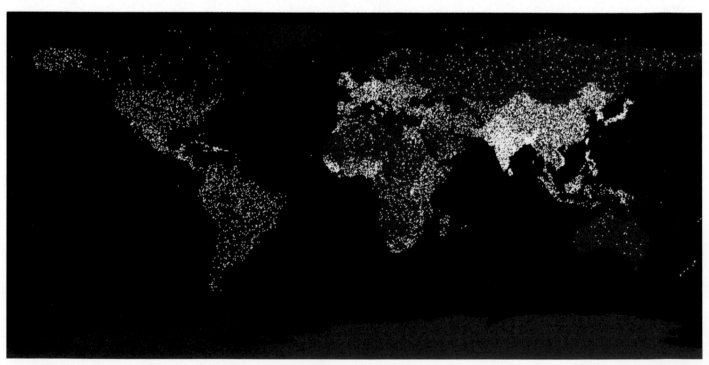

Dot distribution map of world population density (1 dot equals 500,000 people). Enumeration unit: Country.

Question 1: Compare the urbanization pattern in the NASA image with the dot distribution map of population density below. What is the difference in the information in each of the maps?

Question 2: From what you have learned about dot distribution maps in chapter 3, what is the difference in the locational information of the yellow "lights" in the top image, versus the yellow dots in the bottom image?

Question 3: Taken together, what can these two maps tell us about the relationship between lights on the earth and population density? Is this relationship the same across the globe?

The urbanization image was created with a satellite network called the Operational Linescan System (OLS). The satellite sensors in the OLS measure lunar reflection on cloud surfaces, data gathered for use by the Air Force. This reflectance is recorded as a grid of reflectance values in a satellite image. Each of the cells in the grid of a satellite image is called a **pixel,** and each pixel carries information about reflectance intensity for that particular location.

When lunar reflection is at its lowest during the new moon, the sensors are able to collect light emitted from the earth's surface. It is this new moon imagery that Imhoff used to create his global visualization of urbanization.

Using the Image to Assess the Effects of Sprawl

Creating an image of urbanization is one thing, but how can it be used to get a visual understanding of the effects of sprawl? Imhoff's solution was to apply the simple concept of **overlay** from GIS: overlay the global lights data with other georeferenced biological data, such as soil types and vegetation.

To do this, Imhoff's team had to convert the lights image into a GIS data layer by translating intensity of light levels into urban classification levels. Because the nature and extent of the urbanized population varies by region across the globe, the team had to figure out how to convert light intensity into population density for each region separately.

For the United States, they combined the lights image with an overlay of census data showing population density. By comparing the two data layers, they were able to then classify each pixel in the lights image according to whether the intensity indicated urban, peri-urban (small towns and agricultural areas), or non-urban (10 people per square mile or less).

The newly created urban classification data layer was then compared to a data layer classified according to soil-limiting factors. This data layer was derived from the soil types depicted in the UNFAO Digital Soils Map of the World.

By converting the soil types to soil fertility, the scientists were able to create a soil limitations data layer. The portion of this data for the United States is shown on page 142.

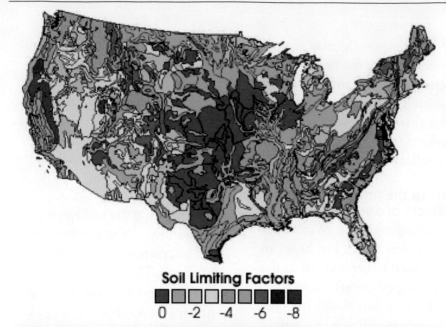

Soil Limiting Factors

0   -2   -4   -6   -8

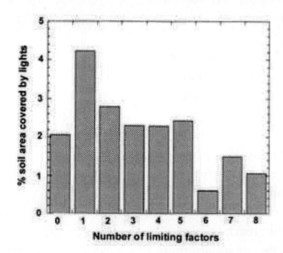

Number of limiting factors

% soil area covered by lights

"Soils Map of the United States" and "Percent of Soil Area Covered by Lights in the United States," by Dr. Marc L. Imhoff, Biospheric Sciences Branch, Goddard Space Flight Center. In Imhoff, Marc L., et al., "Assessing the Impact of Urban Sprawl on Soil Resources in the United States Using Nighttime 'City Lights' Satellite Images and Digital Soils Maps," *Land Use History of North America*, United States Geological Survey (http://biology.usgs.gov/luhna/chap3.html). Used with permission of Dr. Marc L. Imhoff.

In the map on the left, the green areas show a low number of soil-limiting factors, and the red areas show a high number of soil-limiting factors.

Imhoff's team then compared the "Soil Limiting Factors" map to the "City Lights" map to find out how the two types of information compared. Their results are in the bar graph below left.

Question 4: Compare the information in the bar graph to the Soil Limiting Factors map. Which type of soil was found to be most covered by "lights," or most urbanized? Which type of soil is the second-most urbanized?

Question 5: Which type of soil was found to be least urbanized?

Question 6: Which soil types are as a result most threatened by the impact of sprawl? Why do you think this is?

Sprawl also affects soil biodiversity. In its report, Imhoff's team noted: "Our results indicate that four soil types, as classified in the UNFAO system in the United States, may be in danger of disappearing under urban/suburban structures."

Question 7: Compare the "Soil Limiting Factors" map with the inset of the "City Lights" map. Which states seem most likely to be losing soil biodiversity to sprawl?

⟐ 10.3
Planning Urbanization

Mapping **urban morphology** is an ancient geographical problem. A city's structure is defined not only by its layout of streets and the distribution of land use, but also by differences in architecture, roads, views, and infrastructure. Like other large-scale mapping, urban cartography must take into account not one but all of the possible cartographic perspectives: plan, oblique, and profile, each of which provides a different perspective of morphology.

The challenge of mapping urban morphology is even greater when the task is to present a vision of a city that does not yet exist, the potential but as yet invisible **urban landscape.** A good plan should include the streets, buildings, and parks, whether public or private, at correct scale relative to each other, and in such a way that the viewer or reader can imagine exactly how the city will be.

How do you visualize the plan of a city so that it will be accessible to a wide audience, before that city is built? In this section, we will explore an early twentieth century solution to this problem.

In 1909, the Commercial Club of Chicago presented a *Plan of Chicago* by the architects Daniel H. Burnham and Edward H. Bennett, with illustrative plates primarily by Jules Guerin, Fernand Janin, and Bennett. The *Plan* was a sweeping study of proposed changes to the parks, transportation, and neighborhood systems of the city of Chicago, using European cities, such as Paris, Vienna, and Rome, as models.

Below is a conventional map from the *Plan*, showing existing and proposed changes to the region from Grant Park south to the proposed Civic Center. The map is oriented with west at the top, and Lake Michigan and the Grant Park piers at the bottom. Proposed new or widened streets are shown in dark red, proposed parks are shown in light green, and existing parks are dark green. By using color, the design team gives the reader a clear overall sense of the changes proposed to the structure of the city.

But knowing how the structure will be different doesn't give much of an idea of what it will be like to *live* in this new Chicago. Burnham and Bennett wanted to address the latter idea as well, to convey a sense of the new city plan the way one gets a sense of the city while experiencing it directly.

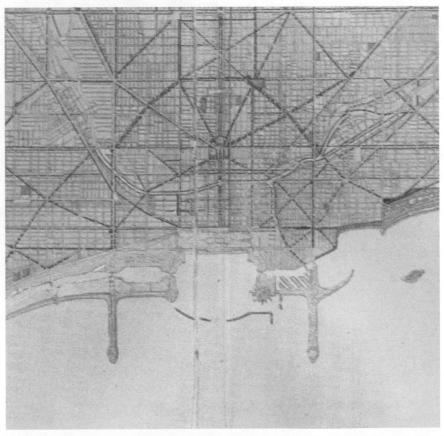

Detail from "Chicago. Plan of the Street and Boulevard System Present and Proposed," in *Plan of Chicago* by Daniel H. Burnham and Edward H. Bennett, Commercial Club of Chicago, 1909.

To enhance the conventional maps, Jules Guerin created aerial and perspective views, landscape sketches, and architectural profiles, creating a massive vision for the city published in a volume of maps similar in format to an atlas. The *Plan of Chicago* was a model of visualization technique before the advent of digital visualization and virtual urban reality. Compare the map on page 143 to the images on these two pages. Each illustration represents portions of the same axis from Grant Park to the proposed Civic Center.

Question 1: How does Guerin use scale to convey a sense of the imagined city?

Question 2: How does he use direction and perspective?

Question 3: What other techniques does Guerin use to bring the proposed urban plan to life? Which elements of the maps are particularly good for conveying a sense of the urban landscape?

Question 4: What elements of the imagined city do you think are unobtainable through maps and views?

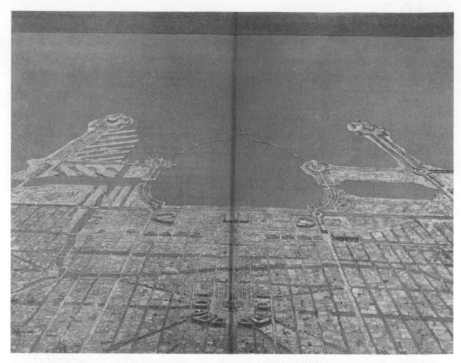

Detail from "Chicago. View of the Proposed Development in the Center of the City, from Twenty-Second Street to Chicago Avenue, Looking Towards the East over the Civic Center to Grant Park and Lake Michigan," in *Plan of Chicago*.

Detail from "Chicago. Bird's-Eye View at Night of Grant Park, the Facade of the City, the Proposed Harbor, and the Lagoons of the Proposed Park on the South Shore," in *Plan of Chicago*.

Detail from "Chicago. Proposed Plaza on Michigan Avenue West of the Field Museum of Natural History in Grant Park, Looking East from the Corner of Jackson Boulevard," in *Plan of Chicago*.

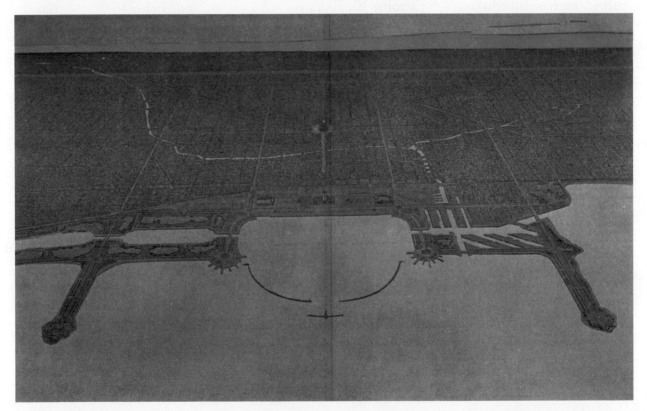

Detail from "Chicago. View Looking West over the City, Showing the Proposed Civic Center, the Grand Axis, Grant Park, and the Harbor," in *Plan of Chicago*.

"Chicago. Section Looking North, Taken through Proposed Grand Axis of the City, Showing the Civic Center and Grant Park," in *Plan of Chicago*.

Sources and Suggested Readings

Urbanization and Hazards

Kayen, R., Collins, B., and Gibbons, H. 2006. USGS scientists investigate New Orleans levees broken by Hurricane Katrina. Sound waves (December 2005 / January 2006). URL http://soundwaves.usgs.gov/2006/01/index.html. Accessed May 16, 2009.

Hurricane Katrina & Rita Clearinghouse Cooperative. LSU CADGIS Research Laboratory. URL http://katrina.lsu.edu/. Accessed May 16, 2009.

Urbanization and Sprawl

Imhoff, Mark L., et al. "Assessing the Impact of Urban Sprawl on Soil Resources in the United States Using Nighttime 'City Lights' Satellite Images and Digital Soils Maps," in United States Geological Survey. *Land Use History of North America.* http://biology.usgs.gov/luhna/chap3.html.

Weier, John. "Bright Lights, Big City." NASA Earth Observatory, October 10, 2000. http://earthobservatory.nasa.gov/Study/Lights/

Planning Urbanization

Burnham, Daniel H., and Edward H. Bennett. *Plan of Chicago.* 1909. Reprint, N.Y.: Da Capo Press, 1970.

Danzer, Gerald A. "The Plan of Chicago by Daniel H. Burnham and Edward H. Bennett: Cartographic and Historical Perspectives," in David Buisseret (ed.). *Envisioning the City: Six Studies in Urban Cartography.* Chicago: University of Chicago Press, 1998, pp. 144–73.

11

The Urban Mosaic

Vocabulary applied in this chapter
path
edge
node
district
landmark
neighborhoods

⊕ 11.1
Feminist GIS, Gender, and Mobility

In Chapter 9, you explored the use of GIS as a tool for analyzing and visualizing geographical data. Although GIS has been demonstrated to be a powerful mapping tool, geographers have also voiced concerns about the limitations of GIS analysis.

Some of these concerns have been voiced by geographers who question the compatibility of GIS—given its traditional reliance on numbers, statistical techniques, and discrete logic—with feminist modes of inquiry. They observe that GIS tools are often used in ways that are not conducive to geographic research about women's lives. Because GIS represents space in a disembodied, planar view (as you learned about in Chapter 2), it diminishes the individual, embodied spaces relevant to daily life.

A few feminist geographers, however, ask whether GIS is only as limited as the uses to which it has been put. We need only redefine and expand our way of using GIS, they say, in order to make it more useful to women. The limitations lie only in our ability to imagine how to use those tools, not in the tools themselves.

What, then, would a feminist GIS look like? This is the question posed by Mei-Po Kwan, who began focusing on a reimagination of the tools of GIS while analyzing how race and gender influence human mobility. Kwan wanted to understand the daily mobility of African American women in the city of Portland, Oregon. She sought to explore those mobilities through a visual and geographical GIS analysis, yet realized that conventional analysis and symbolization were insufficient to communicate her findings.

Rather than reject the digital tools of GIS, Kwan developed a mode of GIS for analyzing women's movement using "life paths." In the life paths, the horizontal locations of the paths measure the routes along which a person travels during the day. The vertical line segments of those same paths indicate the number of hours spent at each location. The taller the line, the longer the amount of time she spends in one place. The more horizontal lines between locations, the more time she spends journeying around the city.

For example, the map below represents her findings for African American women in the city of Portland. The purple life paths can be seen clearly clustered with regard to the outline of the metro area of Portland and the Columbia River. One of the paths marks a trip outside the metropolitan area. North is toward the upper-right corner of the map.

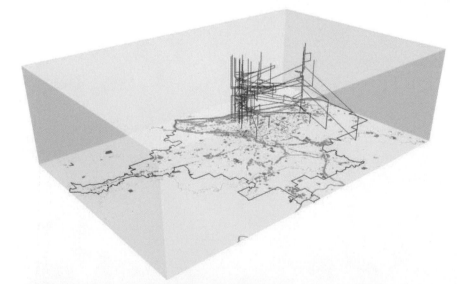

©2002 Mei-Po Kwan. In Kwan, Mei-Po: Feminist visualization: Re-envisioning GIS as a method in feminist geographic research. *Annals of the Association of American Geographers* 92(4), 2002, p. 654 (Figure 1).

In the detail of the next map, Kwan depicts the context of the women's life paths through the downtown area. North is toward the upper-left corner.

***

Question 1: From your reading of the first map, which region of the city do African American women tend to travel within during the day?

Question 2: From your reading of the downtown detail map, how would you describe the pattern of the life paths with regard to the location of downtown Portland and the river?

Question 3: As part of her experimentation with a feminist GIS, Kwan has consciously symbolized this map from an oblique perspective. Why do you think an oblique perspective, as opposed to a planar view, would be preferable to a feminist geographer?

Question 4: If this map were represented through conventional GIS analysis, as two-dimensional lines in a plan perspective, which elements of the information would be lost? How would your understanding of African American women's daily journeys through the city be different?

***

Although life paths tell us how much of a person's day is spent simply moving around the city, the paths tell us little about the nature of those journeys. For example, can the paths also depict a person's emotions? Kwan asked this question in a later study in Columbus, Ohio. For this project, Kwan focused her analysis on the life paths of a Muslim female resident of the city. Kwan sought to understand how Muslim women's lives might have been changed since the September 11 attacks. In a post-9/11 world, what is the experience of a Muslim woman in an American city?

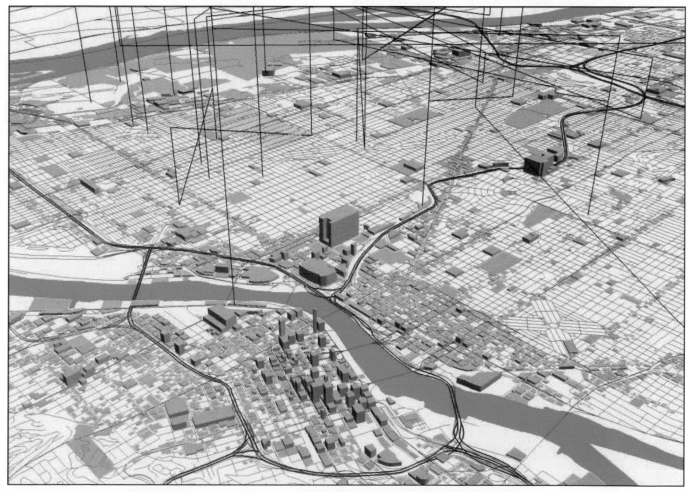

©2002 Mei-Po Kwan. In Kwan, Mei-Po: Feminist visualization: Re-envisioning GIS as a method in feminist geographic research. *Annals of the Association of American Geographers* 92(4), 2002, p. 655 (Figure 2).

Images ©2008 Mei-Po Kwan. From Kwan, Mei-Po: From oral histories to visual narratives: re-presenting the post-September 11 experiences of the Muslim women in the USA. *Social and Cultural Geography* 9(6), 2008, pp. 662–666 (figs 1–4).

Drawing on both locational information as well as video and audio diary transcripts, Kwan made a series of four maps depicting changes over time in one woman's life paths in Columbus, shown above. In the first map, the woman's typical weekday is shown. The second map depicts the same woman's movement in the moments immediately after September 11, and the third map depicts the woman's movements several days later. In the fourth map, the life paths represent one day several weeks later.

Question 5: Describe the differences you see in the four maps. What happens to her path on September 11 and in the next couple of days?

Question 6: In the fourth map, has her travel day returned to normal? In other words, does it resemble her typical day prior to September 11?

@ 11.2
Mapping the Experience of the Cityscape

In Exercise 10.3, you explored the urban plans developed in 1909 by the Commercial Club of Chicago for the *Plan of Chicago*. The *Plan of Chicago* was intended to create a particular mental image of a city that did not yet exist in order to garner widespread public support for large-scale urban development. To achieve this, the cartographers used techniques such as scale, directionality, and perspective to give readers a particular kind of experience when they looked at the maps.

In the 1950s, the geographer and urban planner Kevin Lynch also focused on the connection between peoples' experiences and mental images of the city as a key consideration for urban planning. In his book, *The Image of the City*, he, too, represented those connections with maps. These maps depict the experience of existing cities, first as defined and sketched by the people themselves, then interpreted and compiled into into summary maps by his research team. Since their publication, these maps and the five cognitive elements they present have become a very influential way of interpreting cities.

As you have learned, Lynch found that the way in which people navigate through a city, and the quality of that experience, is greatly influenced by their ability to form a mental image of the city and their relationship to it, what he called the "legibility" of the city. After interviewing people about the way they navigated, Lynch and his team coded their experiences of different spaces according to five structural elements: **paths, edges, districts, nodes,** and **landmarks.**

Question 1: Review what you have learned about these five elements of urban structure. How do each of these elements affect human experience in the city?

Question 2: For each element, what is an example from the city or town where you live?

To summarize the significance of these elements for different cities, Lynch devised a way to symbolize each element in the map, as shown below.

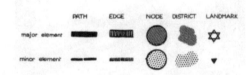

K. Lynch, *The image of the city.* Cambridge: MIT Press, 1960, p.18.

With this custom symbol set, Lynch began mapping urban legibility.

Here, for example, is how the city of Boston appeared when remapped according to interviews with people about their mental image of the city. Notice that, in the legend, the symbols for each element include a subset of symbols representing the percentage of respondents who mentioned this particular element as significant.

Question 3: What streets and places comprise the major paths, landmarks, and nodes of the city of Boston, according to the interviews?

Question 4: Which paths, landmarks, and nodes were mentioned fewer times in the interviews?

Question 5: Where are the edges located?

Question 6: When this research was conducted, the interview subjects were volunteers who lived in the city of Boston. How do you think the map would change if the same interviews were conducted with tourists?

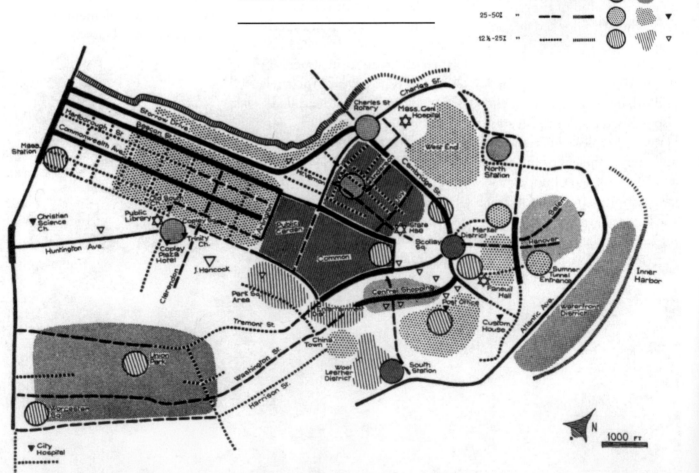

K. Lynch, *The image of the city*. Cambridge: MIT Press, 1960, fig. 35 (p.146).

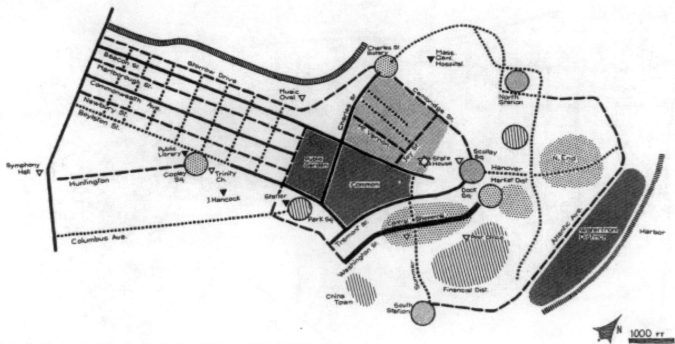

K. Lynch, *The image of the city*. Cambridge: MIT Press, 1960, fig. 36 (p.146).

When Lynch's team asked people to sketch these elements, the maps were different from the interviews. The next map shows how the city of Boston appeared when remapped according to how people sketched the elements of their image of the city.

Question 7: What is the difference in the image of Boston according to interviews and the image of Boston according to sketches?

Question 8: Based on these differences, which streets and places seem most significant to the legibility of Boston?

Question 9: Why do you think people would describe their experience of a city differently when talking about it, as opposed to the way they draw it?

There is a long tradition in human geography of asking people to sketch their environment as one method of interpreting the nature of their experience in that environment. For some geographers, this means providing a person with a base map and asking that person to draw their experiences on the map. When the same base map is used for each person, it can simplify the process of making general statements about people's interactions with their environment in a particular place. In Chapter 1, for example, we examined the way that Hugh Brody used this method for his research on the Doig River Reserve.

Lynch decided not to use the base map method for his own research interpreting people's mental images of their environment. Instead, he asked each person to sketch their own map of the city from scratch, and then compiled all of the sketch maps into one generalized map, as in the map above.

Question 10: Why do you think Lynch wanted interview subjects to sketch without a conventional, printed map as the base? How would such a map change the results of his research?

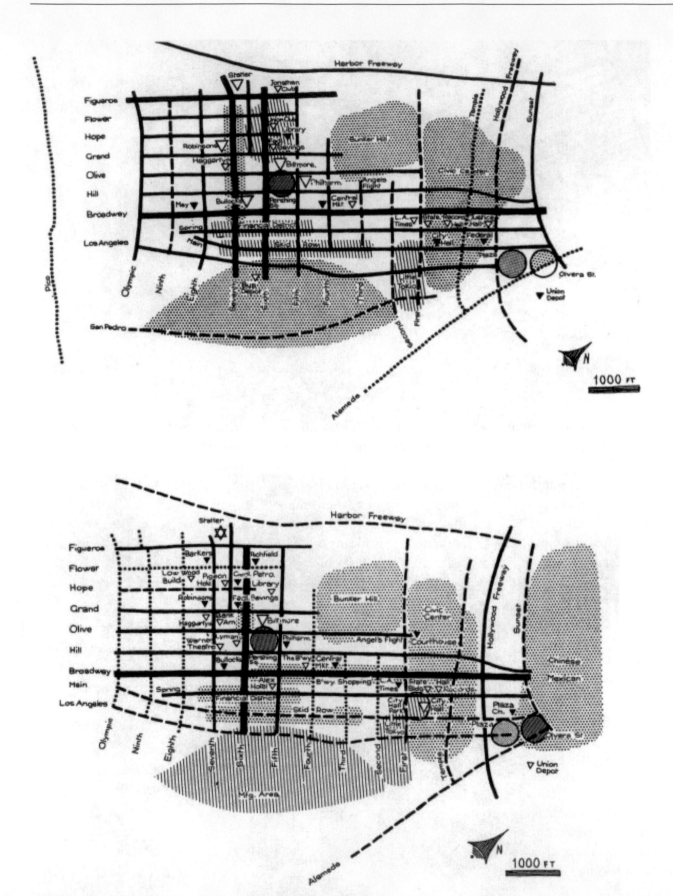

K. Lynch, *The image of the city*. Cambridge: MIT Press, 1960, figs. 43 and 44 (p.150).

Boston was the starting point for Lynch's research, but he also extended the work to Jersey City and Los Angeles. For example, the maps on the opposite page depict the team's summaries for interviews and sketch maps for the city of Los Angeles.

Question 11: Compare the spatial arrangement and hierarchy of the urban elements of Boston and Los Angeles. What differences do you see?

Question 12: Recall that, in the morphology of the city, legibility increases when the five elements are clearly defined. Based on your answer to Question 11, which city is more legible, Boston or Los Angeles? Why?

Question 13: Toward the end of The Image of the City, *Lynch acknowledges that the research did not consider differences in experience based on the subject's gender, race, or economic class. How do you think these characteristics would have influenced this team's findings concerning the legibility of Boston and Los Angeles?*

⊕ ☉ 11.3
The Social Structure of the City

In the 1870s, Charles Booth decided to investigate the social conditions of the London poor through a detailed cartographic inquiry into the spatial distribution of those conditions. Like many of his contemporaries, Booth was troubled not only by the living conditions in London's poor neighborhoods, but also by the limited way in which these conditions were understood.

Dedicated to the combined use of different social scientific methods for the most comprehensive picture of the city, he and his staff set out on what would become more than three decades of map production depicting the interrelationships of demographic statistics for most of the city of London. The results of this sweeping landmark study were the publications between 1889 and 1899 of three series of studies entitled *Life and Labour in London*: the *Poverty Series*, the *Industry Series*, and the *Religious Series*.

In their quest to create a social picture of what was then the largest city in the world, Booth and his staff made use of social data sets available to the public supplemented by their own empirical observations of **neighborhoods** and streets, and participant observation. During the early years of the project, these disparate data sources were combined primarily as written narratives of buildings and neighborhoods. Over time, Booth became more involved in representing these narratives with maps and statistical tables.

Although Booth was not the first to measure London's social conditions through mapping, the maps of *Life and Labour* achieved a level of cartographic detail never before accomplished in urban cartography. Today, the maps stand as a model of the possibilities for social cartography, both in scale and scope.

In this exercise, we will follow Booth's interpretation of the fabric of urban life through distribution mapping as it evolved over time: to record the characteristics of the neighborhoods themselves, to analyze the interrelationships of social forces within those neighborhoods, and to analyze the urban social structure as a whole. To explore how both the city and Booth changed over time, we will look at portions of two of Booth's major maps.

Step 1 To go to the first map, launch your browser and navigate to the "Booth's London Poverty Map" link under the "Exploring Human Geography with Maps" section of the *Human Mosaic* Web site.

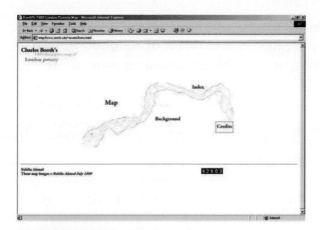

This site, created by Sabiha Ahmad and David Wayne Thomas, is an accessible online version of the first major map to come out of Booth's project in 1889: the "Descriptive Map of London Poverty." The "Descriptive Map" depicts street-scale classifications of wealth and poverty on a street map of London at a scale of 6 inches to a mile.

Step 2 Click on "Map" from the graphic on the main page to go to the clickable map version, titled "Imagemap." You will see the 1889 map in full, with individual squares that can be clicked on to zoom in along the map (as you did to explore Sukula's map in chapter 7). The Thames River cuts a curvy, pale swath through the city, separating the southeast neighborhoods from the northwest neighborhoods.

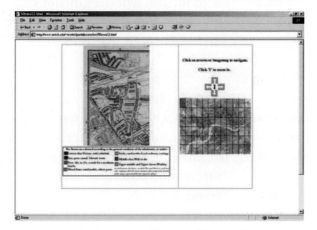

Step 3 Although the grid does not show any reference numbers or letters, Booth's map does have its own index, which runs horizontally from A to M, and vertically from 1 to 12. Click on the upper left corner grid cell to see the layout of the grid: the Web site will link you to the beginning of the grid at A/1-2, as in the bottom image on the right.

Screenshots above courtesy of Dr. David Wayne Thomas, Department of English, University of Michigan.

Step 4 Take a moment to look at the legend, which notes that "The Streets are coloured according to the general conditions of the inhabitants...."

Question 1: What kind of geographical data is this legend portraying? Is it qualitatively different social data, or is the data ranked?

Question 2: How are these characteristics conveyed by the colors Booth has chosen for the map?

From the zoomed-in view, you will see that from here you can also pan in four directions, or zoom in by clicking the "I" at the center of the pan arrows.

Let's jump in and look at Booth's data right in the thick of the city.

Step 5 Using the pan and zoom features of this interactive map, go to cell E/5-6, on the north side of the Thames, and zoom in. You should see Bedford Square in the top portion, and Piccadilly Circus and Trafalgar Square in the bottom portion of the cell.

Question 3: Examine Booth's use of color to depict categories of social status in the neighborhoods. In what way is this technique similar to a choropleth map?

Question 4: As you learned in Chapter 5, in a conventional choropleth map, data is depicted by enumeration unit. In this map, the units are considered "units of analysis"; the information behind the units is not of a strictly numerical nature. What is the unit of analysis used in the map?

Interpreting the Social Character of Neighborhoods
Now that you are more accustomed to the way Booth is symbolizing information, focus on the London social landscape he is portraying.

Question 5: What would you say are the general social conditions around Bedford Square and the British Museum?

Question 6: How do these social conditions change as one moves west? How do they change moving south into Soho?

Step 6 Zoom out, and move to the next grid cell east, F/5-6, and zoom in. You will see Lincoln's Inn Fields at the center and the Thames River in the southeast corner.

Step 7 Imagine that you have just walked east down New Oxford Street from the British Museum, and now you are cutting southeast down to the Strand in F/5-6.

Question 7: How is the social landscape changing? To answer this question, compare for example:

- *Types of workplaces and institutions (public buildings; churches; factories)*
- *Types of transportation, quality and level of roads*
- *Economic class (pattern of poverty and wealth)*
- *Size and quantity of residences*

Question 8: Does it appear that changes in social conditions are gradual in these neighborhoods or abrupt? What kind of pattern in the map indicates this type of change?

Question 9: Try to imagine yourself in each of these neighborhoods. What is it like? For example, which of these neighborhoods are:

> *noisy or quiet?*
> *crowded or deserted?*
> *at which times of day?*

Step 8 Now explore around the rest of the city using your pan and zoom arrows again, to think about and answer the following questions.

Question 10: How do the street structures for the poor classes differ from those of the wealthier classes? Consider the width of the streets, the existence of cul-de-sacs or through streets, and the distribution of alleys and avenues.

Question 11: What is the relationship of the river to the residential pattern? The parks?

Question 12: Are there physical barriers that separate the poor sections from the rest of the city?

A Decade of Change

A decade after the "Descriptive Map" was released, Booth revised and expanded it for the *Religious Series*, indicating changes to the city structure (demolitions and new construction) since 1889, making corrections from the field notes, and supplementing the map with other sketch maps and tables.

The revised map also categorized streets by color according to social conditions, as in the 1889 map. In the new map, however, Booth added church parishes because he wanted to look for the relationship between church parish and poverty.

On page 161 is "The Inner West," one of the sheets of the 1899 map. This portion shows the London neighborhoods south of Hyde Park; Kensington Station can be seen to the left of the center, south of Cromwell Road in Brompton.

This corresponds to the online 1889 map as B–D horizontally, and 7–8 vertically:

	B	C	D
7			
8			

As is clearly shown by the preponderance of yellow, this region of Victorian London was largely wealthy. Part of the significance of Booth's works, however, was the illumination of pockets of poverty and lower income in neighborhoods perceived to be entirely high income.

Step 9 Look back at your online 1889 map and find the corresponding map area according to the diagram above. This region of the map corresponds to three grid cells on the online map.

Question 13: In the 1899 revised map, how does the neighborhood in West Brompton (in St. Luke's parish) compare to that of Wilton Place (in St. Paul's parish)?

Question 14: Compare these same two neighborhoods in your online 1889 map. Have they changed? Why or why not?

Question 15: For both maps, compare the spatial distribution of the "working class" colors to that of the "well-off." Is one income class more densely clustered than the other? How do they differ?

Question 16: Do neighborhoods exist that show both black and red categories in the same block? Which neighborhoods indicate the largest gap between rich and poor?

Question 17: Has each of the income categories changed its distribution pattern? Is there one that has remained relatively similar in its spatial distribution in the city?

Although we can learn a great deal about Victorian London from these maps alone, it is not entirely fair to judge them in this way, as Booth never intended for them to stand alone. In the *Religious Series*, Booth used the color maps in conjunction with sketch maps, statistical tables, and personal observations in his goal to interpret the influence of church districts on London social conditions.

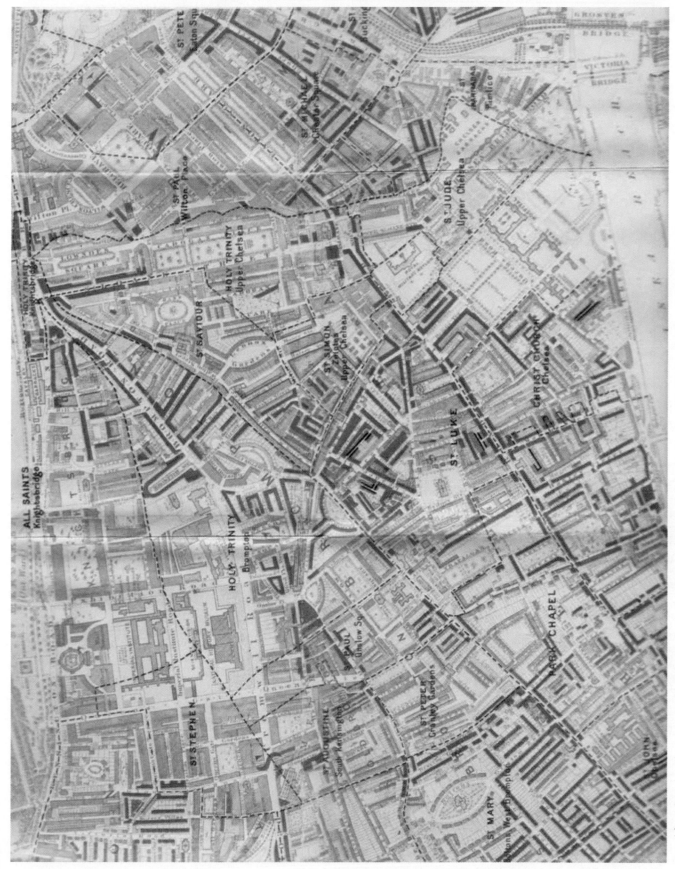

Detail from "Map M—The Inner West" by Charles Booth. In *Life and Labour of the People in London. Third Series: Religious Influences. Vol. 3: The City of London and the West End*, London: Macmillan and Co., 1902.

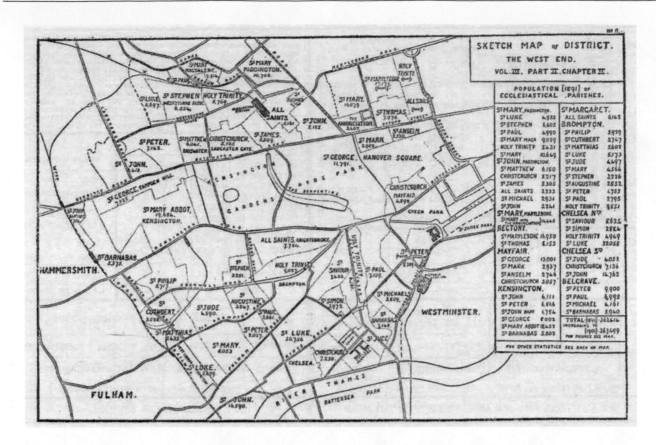

STATISTICS *bearing on the* AREA INCLUDED IN SKETCH MAP NO. II. *Described in Chapter II. (Vol. III., Part II.).*

CENSUS STATISTICS.

Showing Increase or Decrease of Population.

POPULATION IN				**Increase** or Decrease.	
1881.	1891.	1896.	1901.	1881-1891.	1891-1901.
358,647	357,496	367,405	364,133	·29 %	1·86 %

Density of Population.		Age and Sex in 1891.			
1891.	1901.	AGE.	Males.	Females.	Together.
PERSONS PER ACRE. 90·5	92·6	Under 5 years	15,236	15,373	30,609
		5 & under 15 yrs	26,446	27,654	54,100
INHABITED HOUSES. 46,003	43,169	— 20 ,,	14,140	20,745	34,885
		— 25 ,,	16,285	27,946	44,231
PERSONS PER HOUSE. 7·8	8·4	— 35 ,,	27,357	44,205	71,562
		— 45 ,,	19,944	28,179	48,123
NUMBER OF ACRES. 3,948		— 55 ,,	14,275	19,915	34,190
		— 65 ,,	8,865	12,946	21,811
		65 and over	6,812	11,173	17,985
		Totals ...	149,360	208,136	357,496

NOTE.—The district includes MAYFAIR, and part of the BELGRAVE Registration sub-district of St. George, Hanover Square, CHELSEA, BROMPTON, the southern part of KENSINGTON TOWN, a detached portion of ST. MARGARET WESTMINSTER, ST. JOHN and ST. MARY PADDINGTON (except the Ecclesiastical parishes of St. Saviour and St. Peter), and the RECTORY, CAVENDISH SQUARE, and ST. MARY sub-districts of Marylebone (except the ecclesiastical parishes of St. Mark and St. Luke). In these figures the whole of Belgrave is included as well as the four ecclesiastical parishes mentioned above. Cavendish Square (now combined with All Souls) is omitted, as well as the detached parts of St. Margaret and Kensington Town. Owing to these omissions it is probable that the whole area is less crowded than here indicated. For Special Family Enumeration see Appendix.

SPECIAL ENUMERATION FOR THIS INQUIRY (1891).

Sex, Birthplace and Industrial Status of Heads of Families.

SEX.		BIRTHPLACE.		INDUSTRIAL STATUS.			TOTAL HEADS.
Male.	Female.	In London.	Out of London.	Employers	Employees	Neither.	
56,531 71 %	22,745 29 %	29,245 37 %	50,031 63 %	9,801 12 %	47,412 60 %	22,063 28 %	79,276 100 %

Constitution of Families.

HEADS.	Others Occupied.	Unoccupied.	Servants.	TOTAL IN FAMILIES.
79,276 (1·0)	67,100 (·85)	139,879 (1·76)	52,395 (·66)	338,650 (4·27)

SOCIAL CLASSIFICATION according to *Rooms Occupied or Servants Kept.*

	PERSONS.	PER CENT.	
4 or more persons to a room	13,215	3·7	Crowded 25·3 %
3 & under 4 ,, ,,	22,734	6·4	
2 & ,, 3 ,, ,,	54,426	15·2	
1 & ,, 2 ,, ,,	70,168	19·6	
Less than 1 person to a room	12,881	3·6	Not Crowded 74·7 %
Occupying more than 4 rooms	44,132	12·3	
4 or more persons to 1 servant	18,739	5·3	
Less than 4 persons to 1 servant & 4 to 7 persons to 2 servants	16,945	4·7	
All others with 2 or more servants	33,015	9·2	
Servants in families	52,395	14·7	
Inmates of Institutions (including servants)	18,846	5·3	
Total	357,496	100	

Living in Poverty (as estimated in 1889)	17·4 %	100 %
,, in Comfort (,, ,,)	82·6 %	

"Sketch Map of District, the West End" (top), and "Statistics Bearing on the Area Included in Sketch Map No. II" (bottom), from *Life and Labour of the People in London. Third Series: Religious Influences. Vol. 3: The City of London and the West End.*

For example, on page 162 is the sketch and table for the West End.

Question 18: How do the table and sketch map alter your impression of the neighborhoods of the "Inner West," if at all?

Question 19: Do you think Booth could have incorporated the information in the table into the map? Why or why not?

Tip for exploring: If you have two computers side by side (for example, if you are working on this exercise in a computer lab), you can do the steps and questions for "A Decade of Change" completely online, because the 1899 map is also available on an interactive Web site. It will not work on one computer because you need to be able to easily look at both maps side by side, at the same time.

To do the exercise completely online, launch your second browser and navigate to the "Charles Booth Online Archive" link under Exercise 11.3 in the "Exploring Human Geography with Maps" section of the *Human Mosaic* Web site.

At the bullet selection "Poverty Maps of London," click "Search" and select "Wards in 2000."

From the "Browse by Borough" drop-down menu, choose "Kensington and Chelsea" and click "Go."

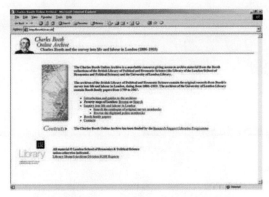

Gateway page of the Charles Booth Online Archive, 2009. © London School of Economics and Political Science. Used with permission.

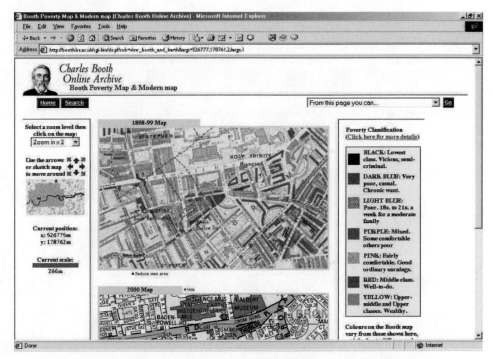

Focus on Brompton from the Charles Booth Online Archive Web site, 2009. © London School of Economics and Political Science. Used with permission.

From the list of Wards, select "Brompton, Kensington and Chelsea," and click the top option, "View on Map."

This will bring you to the Brompton portion of the 1899 map, aligned about exactly with the portion reprinted in this book on page 161, as in the image above.

Uncovering the Dimensions of Race and Class

Charles Booth's community–based sociological scholarship and methods served as inspiration and model for a similar movement of settlement house sociology and cartographic activism in the United States.

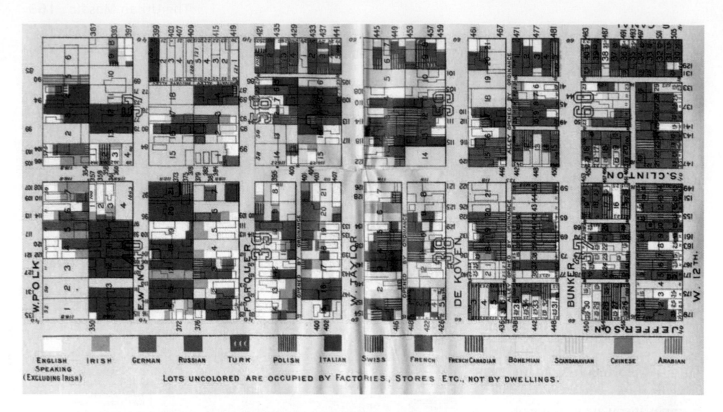

ENGLISH SPEAKING (EXCLUDING IRISH)   IRISH   GERMAN   RUSSIAN   TURK   POLISH   ITALIAN   SWISS   FRENCH   FRENCH CANADIAN   BOHEMIAN   SCANDANAVIAN   CHINESE   ARABIAN

LOTS UNCOLORED ARE OCCUPIED BY FACTORIES, STORES ETC., NOT BY DWELLINGS.

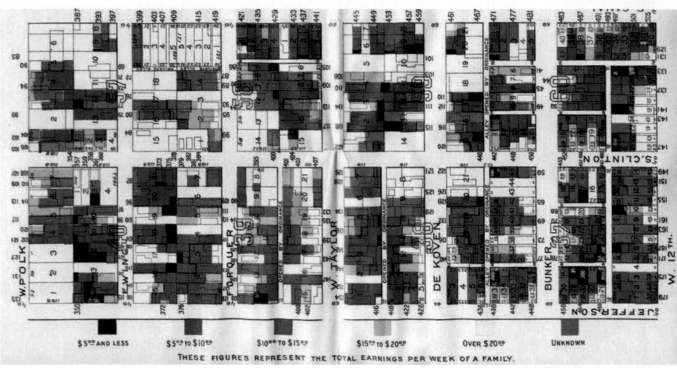

$5.00 AND LESS $5.00 TO $10.00 $10.00 TO $15.00 $15.00 TO $20.00   OVER $20.00   UNKNOWN

THESE FIGURES REPRESENT THE TOTAL EARNINGS PER WEEK OF A FAMILY.

Detail of "Nationalities Map" (top) and "Wages Map" (bottom) in Residents of Hull-House, *Hull-House Maps and Papers*. New York: Thomas Y. Crowell & Co. 1895.

The same year that Booth's "Descriptive Map" was released, Jane Addams founded Hull House in Chicago. In 1895, she published *Hull-House Maps and Papers*, coding the Hull House neighborhood in maps.

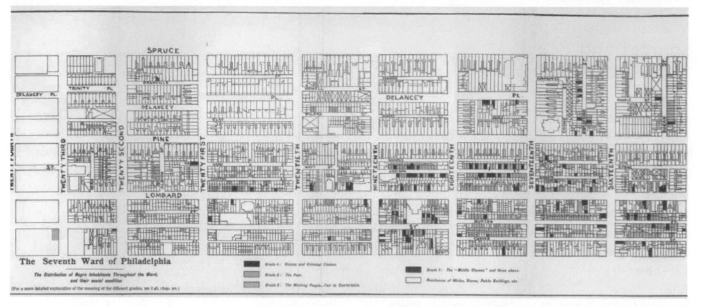

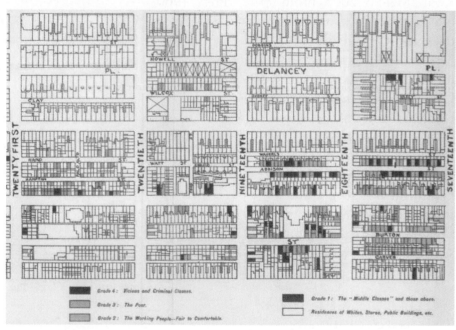

In Philadelphia, W. E. B. DuBois, the first African American awarded a Harvard Ph.D., conducted a community sociological study between 1896-1898. Du Bois also modeled his methods on Booth's work, interviewing all 2,500 households in the Seventh Ward in two years, and coding the results in block-level street maps. The results of Du Bois' study were published in 1899 as *The Philadelphia Negro*.

Question 20: Compare the maps from the two studies led by Addams and Du Bois. What socioeconomic differences existed between these two neighborhoods in Chicago and Philadelphia in the 1890s?

Question 21: Compare the difference between the two legends that Addams and Du Bois established for their studies. For which categories has socioeconomic difference been aggregated, and for which is it mapped in detail? What might explain the choice to aggregate the data differently?

"The Seventh Ward of Philadelphia: The Distribution of Negro Inhabitants Throughout the Ward, and their social condition" (top) and detail (bottom), in Du Bois, W.E.B., *The Philadelphia Negro: A social study*, Philadelphia 1899.

Sources and Suggested Readings

Feminist GIS, Gender, and Mobility

Kwan, Mei-Po. 2002. Feminist visualization: Re-envisioning GIS as a method in feminist geographic research. *Annals of the Association of American Geographers* 92(4):645–61.

Kwan, Mei-Po. 2008. From oral histories to visual narratives: re-presenting the post-September 11 experiences of the Muslim women in the USA. *Social & Cultural Geography* 9(6):653–69.

Pavlovskaya, Marianna and Kevin St. Martin. 2007. Feminism and geographic information systems: from missing object to a mapping subject. *Geography Compass* 1(3):583–606.

Kevin Lynch

Lynch, Kevin. *City Sense and City Design: Writings and projects of Kevin Lynch* (Tridib Banerjee and Michael Southworth, eds.) Cambridge, Mass.: MIT Press, 1990.

Lynch, Kevin. *The Image of the City.* Cambridge, Mass.: MIT Press, 1960.

Lynch, Kevin. *The View from the Road.* Cambridge, Mass.: MIT Press, 1964.

Social Structure of the City

Booth, Charles. *Life and Labour of the People in London. Third Series: Religious Influences. Vol. 3: The City of London and the West End.* N.Y.: Macmillan, 1902.

DuBois, W. E. B. *The Philadelphia Negro—A Social Study.* Philadelphia, 1899.

Residents of Hull-House. *Hull-House Maps and Papers* N.Y.: Thomas Y. Crowell & Co., 1895.

CHAPTER

12

Globalization

Vocabulary applied in this chapter
globalization
Gross Domestic Product
   (GDP)

New vocabulary
cartogram

⊕ ⊛ 12.1
Making Globalization Visible

Globalization is a complex concept to grasp, much less measure or monitor. Most people agree that it is a combination of specific processual and structural shifts in economics, culture, and governance at the global level. These patterns include a shift from industrial to service economies, and from national to global markets, an increasing spread of popular culture and rising consumerism, and a widening gap between the rich and poor.

Question 1: Reflect on the globalization concepts you have learned in class and in your textbook. What other kinds of economic and cultural patterns are indicators of globalization?

Question 2: What are the impacts of these processes on the status and rights of children, women, ethnic minorities, and the environment?

Question 3: What kinds of activities are indicative of political and cultural resistance to globalizing forces?

Throughout this workbook, you have already had glimpses of globalization's visual pattern. For example, in Chapter 2, you analyzed the parallel landscapes of vernacular and modern architecture in Lhasa; in Chapter 4, you compared two contrasting toponymic landscapes in Ireland; and in Chapter 10, you analyzed the location of sprawl. In each of these cases, you were also looking at globalization: both the global effects of forces and structures on people, regions, and landscapes, and local resistance to those effects.

It is one thing to consider globalization as a series of case studies, with separate issues, indicators, and effects. But it is far more difficult to achieve an integrated awareness of globalization, a whole picture of globalization in our head. If we cannot look at it as a whole, how can we monitor it as a whole? Can maps help with this integrated picture?

In this exercise, we will experiment with Worldmapper, an online tool developed by a team of cartographers in the United States and Britain, to assist us with a visual exploration of this complex idea, globalization.

Step 1 Launch your browser and navigate to the "WorldMapper" link under Exercise 12.1 in the "Exploring Human Geography with Maps" section of the *Human Mosaic* Web site. This will take you to the main page for Worldmapper, shown here.

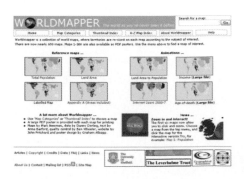

©2006 SASI Group (University of Sheffield) and Mark Newman (University of Michigan).

Worldmapper uses a particular type of thematic map to display geographic information, called a **cartogram.** A cartogram is a map in which the size of each enumeration unit is proportional to the data associated with that unit. Cartograms have no map projection; they are "projected" by the data itself. The resulting map can have a dramatic impact for displaying geographical information over an area, particularly when the larger data values coincide with smaller enumeration units, and vice versa.

That impact, however, comes at a price. Size and shape are distorted to such a degree that other geographic features, such as locations of cities, highways, and hydrography, cannot also be included in the map. If the map reader has little familiarity with the relative sizes of the units, the impact of distortion may be lost. And enumeration units with low data values are often squeezed out of the visual display to make room for the larger data values.

In the case of the Worldmapper cartograms, each cartogram shows a single data set, with regions differentiated by blues, greens, purples, and yellow hues. The enumeration units are countries of the world, so the size of each country is proportional to the data set for that country. Within each region, the data set is repeated in a choropleth display, repeating the information using a sequence of light to dark colors. This technique is called redundant symbols, used here as a means of solving some of the cartogram's interpretation limitations discussed above.

Step 2 From the main page, click on "A-Z Map Index" to navigate to the Index of Maps, as shown above.

©2006 SASI Group (University of Sheffield) and Mark Newman (University of Michigan).

The index displays all maps currently available, directly or indirectly related to globalization, as well as reference maps for comparison. To begin, we will start with one factor considered to be integral to globalization, access to the Internet.

Step 3 Scroll down to "Internet" and click on "Map 335 Internet Users 1990." Worldmapper should generate a new cartogram displaying the number of people in each country who had access to the Internet at any time in 1990.

Step 4 Click directly on the cartogram itself to open a new window with a larger image of the cartogram.

Question 4: What is the pattern of uneven access to the Internet displayed in the cartogram?

Step 5 In the upper-right area of the Web page, click "Next Map >." This will take you to the cartogram based on 2002 data.

Question 5: What is the change in Internet access, at the regional level, during this 12-year period?

Recall from Exercise 7.1 that a choropleth map, to be accurate, must display data as proportional rather than count, because the data is being represented across an area. The same is true for the cartogram. In both the 1990 and 2002 maps, we are looking at the number of people able to access the Internet in each country, not the percent of the population with access. To adjust for this, the cartographers have included a population cartogram as an optional map for comparison.

Step 6 Click the "Open Population Map for comparison" link in the lower right to launch a pop-up population cartogram. Arrange the map on your monitor so you can see both the population and Internet Users 2002 cartograms simultaneously. Make a note of what you observe in these two maps.

Step 7 Close the population pop-up, and click the "Previous map > " link in the upper left to return to Internet Users 1990. Launch the population pop-up for this map as well, and note what you observe.

Question 6: What is the change in country populations, at the regional level, between 1990 and 2002?

Question 7: How do these observations change your assessment in Question 5?

Step 8 Click the "Home" tab in the upper left, to return to the main gateway page for Worldmapper. This time, select the "Internet users 2000–2007" cartogram thumbnail in the Animations section on the right. Worldmapper will launch an animated series depicting the change in the number of Internet users by country over a seven year period.

Question 8: What do you now know about the change in access to the Internet from 1990–2007?

Cartograms in action: Examining the visual dimensions of globalization processes

Step 9 Now that you are comfortable reading the cartograms, click the "A-Z Map Index" link above the animation, to return to the Index.

Obviously, to assemble a map in our mind of globalization and its processes, we need to look at far more than changes in Internet access, or even changes in communication networks.

Step 10 Revisit your response to Question 1. With this answer as a guide, begin to explore the maps available in the Index. For each pattern you identified as an indicator of globalization, choose a map that will give you insight into the geography of this particular phenomenon and examine the corresponding cartogram.

Question 9: Which cartograms are relevant to your indicators from Question 1?

Question 10: For each map, what is the global pattern that you see? What are the regional patterns?

Step 11   For each map that you chose in Step 10, choose a corresponding map which illustrates the impacts of this indicator, and examine the cartograms.

Question 11: For each impact, how does its geography compare to the geographies of indicators you observed in Question 10?

Step 12   Now revisit your answer to Question 3, and choose two maps to explore which portray data sets of resistance.

Question 12: Which two maps did you choose to visualize the geographies of resistance?

Question 13: Compare these two maps to the maps of globalization's process and impacts you have already explored. What trends do you see? How do the regional geographies of resistance contrast to the regional geographies of impacts?

Sources and Suggested Readings

Cartograms

Krygier, John and Denis Wood. *Making Maps: A Visual Guide to Map Design for GIS.* N.Y.: Guilford, 2005.

Dorling, Daniel, Mark Newman, and Anna Burford. *The Atlas of the Real World.* N.Y.: Thames & Hudson, 2008.

ACKNOWLEDGMENTS

Special thanks to our editor Beth McHenry and everyone at W. H. Freeman for their patient support of the second edition, and to Susan David Dwyer for her careful reading of the manuscript. We would also like to thank the following people for their assistance with this book: Jim Biles, Mary Beth Cunha, Mona Domosh, George Erickcek, Stephen Frenkel, Anne Gibson, Michael Hermann, Knud Larsen, Bruce Macdonald, Michael McDonnell, Tim Robinson, Stefan Sarenius, Jonathan Start, Paul Torrens, Bert Vaux, and Kathleen Weesies.

These exercises were created from the library resources of Western Michigan University, Michigan State University, Humboldt State University, and Ohio University. We would also like to thank the departments of geography at Indiana University–Purdue University, Indianapolis, and Ohio University for their support. Finally, a big thank you to Fiona, Jack, and Meredith Dywer for so graciously putting up with several lost weekends.

GENERAL INDEX